A SUSSEX GUIDE

20 SUSSEX CHURCHES

SIMON WATNEY

Illustrated by
SARAH YOUNG

SNAKE RIVER PRESS

SNAKE RIVER PRESS

Book No 1
Books about Sussex for the enthusiast

Published in 2007 by
SNAKE RIVER PRESS
South Downs Way, Alfriston, Sussex BN26 5XW
www.snakeriverpress.co.uk

ISBN 978-1-906022-00-6

This book was conceived, designed and produced by
SNAKE RIVER PRESS

ART DIRECTOR & PUBLISHER *Peter Bridgewater*
EDITORIAL DIRECTOR *Viv Croot*
EDITOR *Robert Yarham*
PAGE MAKEUP *Richard Constable & Chris Morris*
ILLUSTRATOR *Sarah Young*
CONSULTANT *Lorraine Harrison*

This book is typeset in Perpetua & Gill Sans,
two fonts designed by Eric Gill

Printed and bound in China

DEDICATION

To Mrs Barbara Pollard, with love

CONTENTS

INTRODUCTION

*'A church, from long tradition, offers even strangers to
worship a rest from the press of the world'.*

SALLEY VICKERS, *THE OTHER SIDE OF YOU*, FOURTH ESTATE, LONDON, 2006

According to my calculations there are some 533 Anglican churches in
Sussex, of which seven are currently in the care of the hard-pressed
Churches Conservation Trust. Many more face the risk of closure and an
uncertain future. They range greatly in terms of size, date and signifi-
cance throughout the county. The 20 here were chosen for various
reasons, including geographical distribution and the broad sweep of
history. Some I have known all my life, others are new to me. Inevitably
my own likes and dislikes will be felt in these pages, and not everyone
will agree with all my opinions which, of course, is how it should be.

Landscape

Chalk, flint, sandstone and oak – these are the prevailing local materials
of most Sussex churches, and they speak volumes about the underlying
geology of the region. The odd patch here and there of re-used orange
Roman bricks, vast quantities of distantly quarried limestone shipped
upriver from the coast, and innumerable red Victorian bricks in turn tell
of the county's economic history, immediately reflected in its churches.
Roughly rectangular, modern Sussex is some 90 miles wide and some
30 miles deep from north to south. The coastline stretches eastwards
from the low-lying watery dunelands of Chichester harbour to the noble
chalk cliffs at Eastbourne, and on again towards the other-worldly Romney
Marshes. From the north-west spread the fertile central Weald lands, site
of the vast former forest of *Andresweald* (The Undwelt-in-Wood), rising
to the east in the sandy, beech-friendly Ashdown Forest. The underlying
geology is easy to understand, its features running in broad horizontal
bands, eaten away to the south by the constant coastal erosion.

The major features associated most readily with the Sussex landscape
are the South Downs, scooped and ruffled along their northern

escarpments, and creating an unforgettable undulating horizon with small dark woods sheltering in their hollows. Apart from the suburban sprawl behind Brighton, the chalk uplands are still sparsely populated, with small, compact, isolated villages in strong contrast to the pattern of more spread-out inland settlements across the richer Wealden farming-lands reclaimed from the dense primeval forest. This finally succumbed to the hungry furnaces of the iron-smelting industry that flourished from the 16th until the early 19th century. Equally dramatic changes have occurred along the coastline over the centuries as the result of relent-less tidal forces, leaving many one-time ports now land-locked, while others have vanished beneath the waves.

Writing in the 1720s, Daniel Defoe described dense woodlands all along the coast supplying timber to the boat-makers at Shoreham, and shipped to Arundel for transportation on to Woolwich and Deptford and thence to the shipbuilding yards at Chatham in Kent and as far west as Portsmouth. He also noted the prodigious size and quantity of the oak timber grown in the Wealden forests, where 'sometimes a whole summer is not dry enough to make the roads passable'.[1] Near Lewes he recorded a sight:

> which indeed I never saw in any other part of England: Namely [. . .] an ancient lady, and a lady of very good quality [. . .] drawn to church in her coach with six oxen; nor was it done in frolic or humour, but meer necessity, the way being so stiff and deep, that no horses could go in it (ibid.).

In his day the cattle of the Arun valley were considered the largest and fattest in the whole country.

The many place-names that include the suffix 'den', 'hurst' and 'lye' derive from Saxon terms for settlements in man-made clearings in the dense oak forests.[2] Many surviving towns and villages doubtless occupy the sites of far more ancient settlements, and there are still prehistoric stones associated with churches at Aldrington, Alfriston, Shipley, Steyning

---

1. *Daniel Defoe, A Tour Through England and Wales, 1929 ed., p.129.*
2. *Sheila Kaye-Smith, Weald of Kent and Sussex, 1953 ed., p.4.*

and elsewhere. Remote and largely inaccessible for most of their history, many Sussex villages today have no more inhabitants than were recorded in the Domesday survey of 1086. A strong local dialect was recorded in the 18th century by Richard Lower, a schoolmaster from Chiddingly. Its traces survive sporadically in remoter villages and in the recorded legacy of the singing Copper family of Rottingdean, among others.

Christianity in Sussex

Following in the footsteps of Julius Caesar, Sussex was the site of the first Roman incursion led by the Emperor Claudius (*10BCE-AD54*), and supply stations were founded here as early as the first half of the first century AD. Criss-crossed by purpose-built Roman roads, including Stane Street which leads directly from the East Gate of Chichester to London Bridge, the sites of more than 50 Roman villas are recorded. These range from the impressive remains at Fishbourne of the substantial palace built by the Romans for their first client-king, Cogidubnus, ruler of the local Atrebates, to humbler farming settlements, all reflecting a stable and prosperous region from the earliest period onwards.

Little is known about Christianity in Roman Britain, although English bishops attended synods in Gaul and much further afield in the fourth century, suggesting a well-organised church, as elsewhere throughout the Empire. Very little of this survived the withdrawal of the legions in the early fifth century, by the end of which the kingdom of the pagan South Saxons in the west of the county had conquered all the coastal land from Chichester to the Romney Marshes. Standing today inside the surviving walls of the great Roman stronghold at Pevensey, it is painful to think of the recorded siege and massacre here in AD 491, when invading Saxons wiped out the entire local Romano-British population.

St Augustine's mission to Canterbury in AD 597 to re-convert the English made little or no impact in neighbouring Sussex which remained pagan until the eventual conversion of the South Saxons by St Wilfrid in the late seventh century. Indeed, it was the last area of mainland England to become Christian, reflecting its remoteness, and it is surely significant that Wilfrid, a native Northumbrian, arrived by sea.

Selsey was the original cathedral city and the seat of the first bishops until coastal erosion forced the removal of the see inland to Chichester, where the present cathedral was begun in 1091. The port of Bosham was an important late-Saxon centre, its church famously represented in the Bayeux tapestry, and the county's many surviving or partly-surviving late-Saxon churches reflect a flourishing Christian community, especially on the shallow tidal creeks to the west and along the coastal strip and up the lower tidal reaches of the Adur and Arun.

Following the Battle of Hastings the Normans established major resettlements at Lewes, Hastings, Pevensey and Rye. Close to the home-land of the new rulers, the Norman churches of Sussex often have a strong Normandy accent, frequently incorporating older Saxon foun-dations, as at Old Shoreham, Sompting and many other places. To a remarkable degree the borders of modern Sussex closely follow the ancient boundaries of the Christian Diocese founded by St Wilfrid in AD 681. The Domesday survey lists 92 churches in the county, of which most were in the centre and west. By 1517, this had risen to 278.

Of the comparatively few abbeys in the county, Battle was the richest, and the early Cluniac foundation at Lewes the most architecturally impor-tant. The survival of the exquisite Tournai-marble tomb-slab of its co-founder, the Countess Gundrada de Warrenne, now inside the later church of St John the Baptist at Southover, suggests something of the enormity of what was sacrificed to the rapacious greed of Henry VIII. The Cistercians settled at Robertsbridge while the Franciscans, as usual, preferred established towns including Lewes, Chichester and Winchelsea. Later collegiate foundations were built at Boxgrove, Hastings, Steyning and elsewhere.

Sussex is a county of very few saints, reflecting its geographic and cultural remoteness from the rest of the country. The few that there are include St Cuthman of Steyning, whose sanctity was entirely rustic, the obscure martyr-saint Lewinna of Alfriston, whose relics were stolen by a French monk and taken to France in the 11th century, and St Richard of Chichester, whose virtues, it has to be said, were largely administrative and political.

Churches

The pattern of Sussex churches provides a faithful map of the history of the county as a whole. Many, such as Bishopstone, Sompting and Worth, retain substantial late-Saxon features, especially along the coastal strip and up its navigable river estuaries. The Normans established their power through new castles and often mighty churches, sometimes adding to earlier structures and sometimes building from scratch. Such new churches vary from the humble and remote, as at Coombes and Ford, to those built on a much grander scale, as at New Shoreham, St Mary's Eastbourne, and so on.

Many Sussex churches are small and of one build, suggesting much about the relative backwardness and poverty of the region as a whole, where there was generally little money for rebuilding, or population pressure requiring enlargements. Others are more typical slow-growth buildings, especially in the larger seaports and market-towns where leading families, guilds and others regularly constructed new aisles and chapels, or rebuilt older parts in keeping with more up-to-date styles as funds became available. Almost every church was originally associated with an adjacent manor house where many generations of individual families lived, only to be replaced by others when they moved away or died out. Such leading local families frequently expressed their piety with gifts of new fittings and furnishings including roofs, altars, stained glass, screens and so on, as well as their own funeral monuments.

For a thousand years churches have played a central role in local community life, and in the lives of individuals which were invariably organised around the celebration of the sacraments and the great annual festivals of the Christian year, including saints' days. Marriage, baptism, and funerals lay at the heart of people's lives, and every church was closely associated with these central rites of passage. All churches include different areas with differing uses; until the Reformation the west end generally belonged to the parishioners while the east end was maintained by the clergy for religious ceremonies. It is thus unhelpful to talk about their architecture as if this could somehow be entirely separated from their contents, especially the many ritual-objects they contain, including altars, fonts, pulpits, screens and so on. Usually locally made, these often provide important and beautiful examples of specialised craft skills including carpentry, wood- and stone-carving, wall-painting and so on, the more precious for running against the grain of modern mechanical mass-production and its associated lowering of aesthetic standards and sensitivities.

Churches are frequently the oldest surviving monuments in any landscape, and their baptismal fonts are often older still, dating from the very earliest period in a church's history, of which they are sometimes the only visibly surviving physical feature. Sussex has a great number of ancient fonts, ranging from the many plain early-Norman limestone tub-shaped examples found at Racton, West Wittering and elsewhere, and the rarer goblet-shaped examples at North Stoke and East Marden, to the later Norman Purbeck-marble fonts imported by sea from Dorset. These are usually square as at Amberley, and occasionally octagonal as at Bosham. Most have plain arcading along their sides but others are more richly decorated as at New Shoreham. The history of fonts provides its own fascinating picture of slowly changing tastes, from the noble simplicity of so many early examples to the more elaborately carved ones at Boxgrove and Willingdon.[3] Sadly, many were destroyed or badly damaged during the Reformation and Civil War, only to be replaced later in the 17th century as at Ashburnham and Withyham. The evolving history of baptism is equally reflected in the fine later examples at Glynde, St Andrew's in Hove and St Bartholomew in Brighton.

The different types of decorative tracery used in windows and on screens and many other furnishings also embody the history of the changing cultural climate over the centuries, enabling one to confidently date furniture or monuments or parts of whole buildings. Every element of a church has its own richly rewarding history, from the carving of capitals to the evolving shape of bells or the design of spires and gravestones. Monuments have their own particularly important place in most churches, and range from relatively small brasses or tablets to much

---

3. *Maud F. Drummond Roberts, Some Sussex Fonts Photographed and Described, 1935.*

grander standing wall-monuments, memorial-windows and so on. The endlessly unpredictable and surprising physical relations between monuments and other church furnishings, often in the architectural context for which they were made, provides one of the most enjoyable aspects of church-visiting. Closely tied to the spirit of their period, they frequently speak eloquently of the complex individuals they were designed to commemorate and afford a sharp reminder of the central role such individuals played at every level of local and national history. They are also often wonderful works of art in their own right, reflecting slowly changing cultural tastes and patterns of belief about the afterlife. Taken together, church monuments form much the most important body of English sculpture in endlessly fascinating sequences and combinations from different centuries.

There is no substitute for the direct first-hand experience of looking closely at monuments and other church fittings and furnishings *in situ*. Their variety may seem bewildering, but one soon develops an eye for materials and historical periods, and indeed for individual workshops. Books cannot begin to describe the quality of light on alabaster quarried from different English sites, or the quality of original 15th-century stained glass compared to, say, early 17th-century painted glass.

The timescale of most churches is measured in centuries. As at Boxgrove and Coombes, they sometimes stand in landscapes which have changed comparatively little since they were first built, while others find themselves in new surroundings. Thus at North Stoke the church is all that now survives of the entire busy settlement which it formerly served, and Winchelsea church is now itself a monument to the largely vanished but once thriving port over which it proudly presided for so long. Other churches, once entirely rural as at Hangleton and Patcham, now find themselves enveloped in subsequent suburban sprawl. Invariably the wider landscape is mediated by surrounding churchyards which provide their own distinct pleasures, offering refuge to wildlife and visitors alike. The iron-smelting industry which decimated the great oak forests of the Weald in less than 300 years is reflected in many delightful surviving 17th- and 18th-century cast-iron headstones, especially in the north of the county. These are often very like contemporary fire-backs and were doubtless designed and cast in the same workshops.

Deeply embedded in their various landscapes and townscapes, parish churches provide a uniquely intimate introduction to regional and national history. The importance of churches as symbols of real and not merely imagined historical continuity cannot be sufficiently emphasised. There is much talk these days of declining congregations, but this is hardly new and was indeed a commonplace of Victorian commentary. However harshly we may sometimes judge overzealous 19th-century church restorers, they were at least committed to the long-term future of the buildings they often so misguidedly transformed. Our parish churches face a greater threat today than at any time in their history, and the wishes and needs of the people who visit churches for many different personal reasons should be taken very seriously.

These may range from entirely private spiritual emotions to a wide variety of historical and artistic interests, and of course many church-visitors arrive with mixed or unclear motives. Certainly church-going in modern Britain should not be exclusively defined in terms of the numbers of bums on seats at services, not least because supposedly 'casual' visitors may frequently outnumber regular Christian worshippers. In this context we surely need to expand what we mean by acts of worship. For if, as Alan Billings has recently suggested, Christian ministry is 'about meeting a pastoral need by making the grace of God concrete for people',[4] then the question of the accessibility of churches should be recognised as a basic aspect of religious ministry and witness. This seems closely connected to the idea of pilgrimage in the modern world, memorably defined by the great Sussex writer Hilaire Belloc[5] as,

> a nobler kind of travel, in which, according to our age and inclination, we
> tell our tales, or draw our pictures, or compose our songs . . . a separate and
> human satisfaction of a need, the fulfilling of an instinct in us, the realization
> of imagined horizons, the reaching of a goal.

---

4. *Alan Billings, Secular Lives, Sacred Hearts, the role of the church in a time of no religion, 2004.*
5. *Hilaire Belloc, The Idea of Pilgrimage, Hills and the Sea, 1906.*

In reality, degrees of access to churches vary considerably. The permanent locking of churches is usually justified in terms of stated anxieties about theft and vandalism, but these would never be used to defend the closure of parks or museums or indeed shops. Such apologists seem wilfully unaware of the great number of churches that are happily open within reasonable hours. In all of this we may note the regrettable modern tendency to regard churches as liabilities rather than indispensable resources which lie at the very heart of Christian culture and our national history. Nothing shocked me more in the writing of this book than the discovery that the most important 20th-century church in all Sussex, namely the former church of St Wilfrid at Elm Grove in Brighton had been converted into flats as recently as 1992, despite vigorous protests by local parishioners. To these, and to its Grade II listing, the Church Commissioners had proved sadly impervious.

In this context, one should also note the very varied quality of parish websites which range from the excellent to those such as Cuckfield where at the time of writing there is not so much as a mention of the church or its history, in strong contrast to the Willingdon website, where it is made clear that the parish sees 'the church as a sacred space for all people. God's space in the midst of often very hectic lives – and it is here for you'. The sense of welcome is palpable.

Finally, it should be emphasised that one's understanding of churches benefits incalculably from revisiting them at different times of day and year, in different lights and weathers, and at different stages of one's own life. Some people are passionately interested in bells, and others in stained glass or monuments or in wider questions of genealogy or local history, or simply in getting away for a few precious moments from the frantic pressures of modern life. All are equally valid reasons for wanting to visit churches. How many people gladly troop off to look at churches in France and Italy yet rarely, if ever, consider entering churches much closer at hand? Public transport remains reliable throughout the county and the best way to start or finish any visit remains as Belloc recommends, on foot, 'with the sky above one, and the road beneath, and the world on every side, and time to see all' (*ibid*).

Architecture and History

Although we are not often aware of it, we all use specialist language every day in relation to skills and interests central to our lives, if not to everyone else's. Certainly the specialist language of architecture can seem rather intimidating to the uninitiated, but not for long.

Like every other enduring field of human creative imagination and mechanical ingenuity, architecture embodies the changing expression of successive ages. Yet most people walk about without any very accurate sense of the dates of any of the buildings around them, having been systematically denied the opportunity in schools or elsewhere of understanding anything very much about the daily lives of their own direct ancestors. The history of kings and queens is endlessly fascinating with its larger-than-life depictions of every kind of human frailty and achievement, but there are also other, at least equally important, ways of sensing historical time, of which perhaps the most telling concerns our awareness of the literal fabric of the past. We can experience this physically embodied in constantly changing art and design, from clothes and furniture to entire buildings.

The same history is reflected in a particularly glorious and often life-affirming way in church art of all kinds, the making of which involved technical skills with their own distinct if often over-lapping histories, locating us directly in relation to the earlier inhabitants of these islands in an unbroken sequence of human artefacts and vision. Such understanding of the ever-changing look of the past also helps locate us in relation to the rest of Europe and the world beyond, in our growing awareness of the constant dialogue and interaction with different European cultures which informs every aspect of the history of our churches and their often remarkable contents.

One of the most important concrete benefits to be derived from the process of becoming familiar with the broad sequence of changing architectural styles is the way this level of visual knowledge firmly anchors one in continuous historical time. Among many other things, visiting churches can provide a particularly enriching way of integrating one's own life into the history of one's locality and the wider world.

Writing this book, I have not assumed any necessary prior acquaintance with church architecture, and a glossary of specialist terms is provided on p.88. I have also provided a list of useful websites on related topics, and a bibliography of books and articles on which I have drawn in my own research, and from which I occasionally quote. Hopefully these will encourage more people to visit churches more regularly, not least because there are always things to discover which are not included in available guide books or other historical accounts. Most published church guides are generally trustworthy, though modern research sometimes challenges long-cherished local legends, such as those concerning the occupants of the great sequence of early 14th-century tombs at St Thomas, Winchelsea.[6] To a surprising extent there are still remarkable discoveries to be made, including not least the sense of the sacred, and of our own historical belonging.

Conclusion

Parish churches remain highly vulnerable to the vicissitudes of taste and changing circumstances, and as I write the future of many Sussex churches is precarious, including several important buildings in Brighton, a city with one of the worst conservation records in Britain. It is fashionable these days to talk dismissively of the so-called 'heritage industry', yet in reality important churches continue to be demolished or irreparably damaged throughout the country.

Needless to say not everything can or should be saved, but our ecclesiastical heritage is unique and deserves much better recognition and protection than it currently receives. Sadly the Church of England cannot always be relied upon to sustain the great tradition of responsible stewardship with which it is still widely and often mistakenly associated. The survival of all the churches described in these pages reflects the care of countless local incumbents and parishioners over the centuries, and the least we owe them is to honour their commitment to the long-term historical vision by which they were inspired.

---

6. Blair, Goodall & Lankester, The Winchelsea Tombs Reconsidered, Church Monuments, Vol XV, 2000, pp.5-31.

ST MICHAEL

AMBERLEY

Perched on its own small escarpment, the picturesque village of Amberley looks out on one side over the Sussex Weald towards the North Downs and on the other southwards across the Wildbrooks, the wetlands of the Arun valley, less wet these days since the river was embanked. The church of St Michael stands just outside the 14th-century castle walls built to enclose an older fortified manor house founded by the Bishops of Chichester and nowadays an hotel. Patched outside with stone and flint, the present church dates from around 1140, with a south aisle which was probably added at the very end of the 12th century, together with a new roof sweeping down to cover both the nave and the aisle. The sturdy west tower was added in the 13th century when the chancel was rebuilt with a typically under-stated Early English-style triple-lancet east window, and side lancets. Inside the south porch the early 14th-century doorway has well-carved capitals decorated with oak, hawthorn and vine leaves.

The most dramatic and memorable feature at Amberley is the tall Norman chancel arch with four bands of energetically zig-zagging chevrons of different widths moving in different directions to very exciting effect. It rests on large stylised leafy capitals, with a single small, cat-like animal-head on the south-east side facing the main altar. The nave windows also have nice upright abstract leafy capitals like those flanking the chancel arch. Together with the decoration of the nave capitals and arches, this is similar to contemporary work at Steyning. Standing against the west side of the first pier of the south nave arcade is a large, square font typical of the late 12th century. Damaged in various moves, it is decorated with shallow blank arches, four on each side, and rests on a modern slab above a drum with four modern corner colonettes.

Sadly, much wall painting was destroyed during the misguided restoration of the 1860s, when large areas of medieval plaster were painstakingly chipped away, as in so many other English churches, but fortunately a substantial area remains on the south side of the chancel arch. Although badly faded, this shows Christ in Majesty above the Passion-story, including the Flagellation, the Procession to Calvary, the Crucifixion and the Resurrection. Until around 1865, the most prominent painting in the church was a painted figure of Christ seated on the lap of the Virgin Mary, with a kneeling ecclesiastic below. This was located on the north side of the east end of the south aisle, but of this there is sadly no longer any trace. It is not clear from the old description whether it was a form of pietà or a Madonna and Child.[1] On the south wall of the aisle, however, there is still a tiny 14th-century detail from the Visitation showing the heads of St Mary and St Ann. Although much restored, this tends to confirm the suggestion that there was a Lady Chapel at this end of the aisle.[2] On the south side of the east end of the aisle is a faded biblical text painted after the Reformation on top of an earlier scene.

Besides a well-designed brass to John Wantelle (*died 1424*), now displayed on the east wall of the south aisle, and a few slabs now in the porch, there are no old monuments at Amberley. In 1530 local farmer George Rose left instructions for the construction of a tomb by the north door, to be 'paynted wt a crucifixe and my picture, wt my 11 children', but no trace of this, nor any other old monuments, survived the combined effects of the Reformation, the Civil War and the work of Victorian restoration.[3] Four modest 18th-century tablets cling to the outside of the east wall of the church whence they were exiled in the

1. *The Revd. G.A. Clarkson, Notes on Amberley, its Castle, Church etc, 1865, p.185-239.*

2. *Nigel Foxell, Amberley Church-A Critical Appreciation, 2006.*

3. *E.N. Staines, Dear Amberley; A guide to Amberley and the History of the Parish, 1968, p.36.*

19th century, and there are a few Victorian epitaphs. The best monument is a small tablet at the west end by Eric Gill (*1882-1940*), commemorating Joan Stratton, who died aged 17 in 1919, with typically good lettering and a sensitive portrait roundel in low relief.

An early 19th-century drawing shows the interior of the church with the lower section of the medieval chancel screen intact with its original doors, together with a full complement of box-pews and a fine 17th-century two-decker pulpit, but this was all swept away in the 1860s, the pews apparently re-used as pig-troughs. The magnificent open kingpost roof was also boarded over at this time, but was opened up in the early 1960s, when the old Horsham-stone roofing was replaced with tiles.

In the south aisle is a beautiful two-light window by Veronica Whall (*1887-1970*) commemorating Edith Jennings (*died 1931*) with St Edith and two angels. The best glass at Amberley is set into the arch of the former Norman doorway on the north side of the nave. Designed and made by Robert Anning Bell (*1863-1933*), it commemorates his friend the artist Edward Stott (*1855-1918*) who lived locally. One of the very best windows in Sussex, it demonstrates the way in which late Pre-Raphaelite taste led to our native form of Art Nouveau. Depicting the Entombment of Christ in a border of demi-angels with animal vignettes along the bottom, the central image derives from a painting by Stott based on Titian's celebrated version of the subject in the Louvre, rethought here in nervily intense early 20th-century terms.

Stott is buried on the west side of the churchyard where there is a substantial carved upright stone monument with a lively bust on top and a delightful relief-medallion of the Boethian hunter Orion playing a lyre, a perfect embodiment of the haunting mood of Edwardian neo-paganism one associates with the woodcuts of Gwen Raverat and the short stories of Arthur Machen. By the sculptor Francis Derwent Wood (*1871-1926*), it is showing ominous signs of weathering.

Getting there   National grid ref. TQ027132

❱ Amberley is 4 miles (6 kilometres) north of Arundel, just off the B2139.

❱ Amberley train station is on the London-Chichester line.

❱ Open daily. Details on Diocesan website: **www.diochi.org.uk**

ST PETER

ASHBURNHAM

At first sight St Peter at Ashburnham in East Sussex appears to be a typical late-medieval Perpendicular church, but it was in fact re-built in 1665, although retaining the 14th-century west tower from an earlier building. As soon as you begin to look at the details the date becomes more apparent, and it is instructive to compare the lozenge decoration on the north porch to that on the west door at St Mary the Virgin in Goudhurst a little way across the border in Kent, which dates from around 1638. The well-preserved Restoration interior is characteristically cool yet magnificent, with a plain wooden pulpit, a west gallery raised on Ionic columns, and box-pews. There is also a fine large pedimented reredos from the 1670s now positioned on the north wall of the nave. It has paintings of Moses and Aaron in a wooden frame, with superbly carved cherubs and winged angel-heads, recently picked out in gloss white paint, to sadly disfiguring effect. Of a similar date is the large, highly unusual font with an octagonal bowl on top of a big square pyramidal stepped stem. It is so eccentric one suspects the hand of the sculptor John Bushnell is associated with it, especially given his work here in the 1670s. It has a pretty wooden pierced ogee-ribbed cover.

St Peter was the mausoleum church of the Ashburnham family who lived here from the 12th century until the line died out in 1953. The magnificent adjacent mansion was largely demolished between 1959 and 1961 after a fire, and only a squat reminder of its former magnificence remains as a conference centre. The family is commemorated by two major tombs, the earlier of which is that of John Ashburnham (*died 1671*) and his immediate family. He was the builder of the church and a loyal favourite of Charles I, by whom he was nicknamed Jacko. Set against the east end of the north wall of the north chancel chapel, it is grand yet reticent and very much in the classical courtly style established by the London- and Amsterdam-trained mason-sculptor Nicholas Stone in the early 17th century. Positioned against a large, plain, upright rectangular black back-plate, it consists of a noble canopied marble reredos with a large white pediment supported on black Corinthian columns.

On top is a superbly carved escutcheon proudly proclaiming the family's ancestry, while at ground-level is a beautiful white marble tomb-chest standing on a white plinth raised on a black step, with two groups of small kneeling figures in relief facing one another on the front. Many of their hands are later replacements. On top of the chest is a polished black lid carrying three excellent traditional recumbent white marble effigies with their heads resting on tasselled pillows. He lies in the middle, with his first wife behind him wearing a wimple and a long shroud-like robe, and his second wife in front of him in contemporary dress with long ringlets, and wearing a coronet. All three have their hands together in prayer, those of his first wife also being later replacements.

The kneelers are conceived entirely within a Jacobean convention that was already old-fashioned by the eve of the Civil War, but which took on a new lease of life after the Restoration as an emblem of continuity with the past across the great chasm of the Interregnum. The monument is surely from the same hand as that commemorating Henry, Ninth Earl of Kent, and Lady Arabella, Countess Dowager of Kent, in the De Grey mausoleum at St John The Baptist at Flitton in Bedfordshire, and the monument to Sir John Evelyn at St Nicholas at Godstone in Surrey, the latter being generally accepted as the work of the sculptor Thomas Burman (*1617-74*).

An attribution to Burman is reinforced by the presence of a white marble cartouche set horizontally on top of the tomb-chest to the left of the effigies' heads, a technique strongly associated with the workshop of Nicholas Stone, for whose son, John Stone, Burman had worked in the 1650s. Burman had originally been trained under the leading London-based mason-sculptor Edward Marshall, whose work may be seen at Horsham, and his influence is felt here in the rather streamlined quality of the effigies. The attribution is further supported by the fact that Burman's most celebrated pupil, John Bushnell, was responsible for the other great monument at Ashburnham, made shortly after his former master's death, suggesting that he may well have inherited the commission, despite a dramatic earlier falling out between the two men. Certainly Bushnell seems also to have taken over another commission at West Dean in Wiltshire after Burman's death.

The second great monument occupies the entire west side of the north chapel and commemorates William Ashburnham who died in 1679, together with his wife Jane, formerly the Countess of Marlborough. Although not himself ennobled, William had royal connections. Born sometime before 1620, he was the son of Sir John Ashburnham (*c.1572-1620*), had served as a Major-General in the royalist army of Charles II, was Colonel General of the county of Dorset and served as the king's cofferer, or treasurer. Very much a sister to Bushnell's earlier monument at All Saints, Fulham to John, Viscount Mordaunt, Ashburnham's fittingly ornate memorial is set against a huge, plain, dark grey marble background, and takes the form of a grand theatrical tableau, set on its own wide stage raised by two steps, on which stands an enormous pale grey marble sarcophagus with a polished black marble lid. The inscription on the front is in a scrolly frame with scary open-mouthed beast-masks above and below, and is very typical of Bushnell. On top of the lid are two white marble effigies, she demurely semi-reclining on the left, he kneeling on the right with his hands stretched out despairingly. He is however conceived and executed on a different, larger scale to her, creating a most unsettling psychological effect which is further reinforced by the presence of a very anatomically challenged cherub hovering above her head with a wreath.

At the front corners of the slab are two free-standing plinths which echo the profile of the sarcophagus, and support a small white coronet on the left, and a plumed helm on the right. Behind the figures is a flat white marble curtain under a big baldacchino held open at the sides by two startlingly inept cherub heads. The quality of carving is wildly uneven and, while the initial general effect is magnificent, the cherubs verge on the monstrous. If one looks more closely, the detail is very mad indeed, as is so often the case with Bushnell. The sarcophagus, however, is a fabulous piece of Mannerist invention, and the individual elements (helm, coronet, etc.) resting on their bulgy black plinths are of the greatest beauty and strangeness.

Getting there   National grid ref. TQ689145
◉ Ashburnham is 4 miles (6 kilometres) from Battle just off the A271 to Bexhill. There are buses from both towns.
◉ Open by arrangement with the Revd. S. R. Talbot, tel. 01424 893605.
◉ Details on Diocesan website: **www.diochi.org.uk**

BOXGROVE PRIORY

BOXGROVE

Surrounded by a working farming landscape some little way to the east of the village from which it takes its name, Boxgrove Priory is approached past the melancholy ruins of its former Norman nave and monastic buildings. The Benedictines settled here in the early years of the 12th century and their grand cruciform church was completed around 1165, when the eastern arm was extended. In the early years of the 13th century the aisled choir was enlarged, and happily the entire east end, together with the earlier central tower and transepts, survived the Reformation to become the present parish church of St Mary and St Blaise. The piers of the two surviving bays of the nave and crossing area have subtly varied scalloped capitals, and there are several excellent Norman head-stops which should be compared to the badly weathered human and animal heads of an earlier date on the outside corbel-table. Look out for the beautiful blank arcading high up under the tower, with some very abstract leafy capitals, like those on the chancel arch at Amberley.

Taking its lead from the retrochoir of nearby Chichester Cathedral, the choir at Boxgrove is a superb example of Early English architecture, the name given to the style which gradually introduced pointed arches, opting for effects of noble simplicity in reaction to the wilder aspects of late Romanesque decoration with all its splendidly frenzied zig-zags and love of surface decoration. In the choir at Boxgrove one senses a profound change of historical mood reflected in a newly emerging architectural language. This is most apparent in the huge, severely plain three-light east window which is viewed in the context of the bouncing rhythm of the flanking choir arcades with their big, paired, pointed arches under huge over-arching rounded mouldings. The cool prevailing limestone contrasts splendidly with the dark polished Purbeck marble. The older style of dog-tooth decoration is used, but sparingly, rather like a farewell performance by a much-loved decorative feature which the architect couldn't quite bear to part with.

At the same time, distinctive buttresses were pushed out across the roofs of the choir aisles to counter the thrust of the vault above, which benefits from the charming 16th-century painted decoration by local artist Lambert Barnard, who also decorated the Lady Chapel vault in Chichester Cathedral. Although their forms may be rather rustic and unsophisticated, their overall delicate decorative sense is unerring, and Barnard clearly recognised that any kind of mechanical repetition of motifs would have been completely out of place. While looking upwards, don't miss the superb roof-boss at the east end of the vault with eight faces in a circle. This is clearly from the same hand responsible for the boss in the south choir aisle of Chichester Cathedral, which has six identical faces with leaves sprouting from their mouths. The lower part of the west wall incorporates some parts of the pulpitum with both its doorways blocked since the nave to which they formerly gave access had its roof removed.

One senses that Boxgrove never really recovered from the shock of the dissolution of the monasteries. There are surprisingly few old fittings and hardly any monuments. Or were these swept away in the 19th century? Certainly architect George Gilbert Scott (*1811-88*) was given carte blanche to get rid of anything he thought 'unworthy' at the time of his restoration work, when the Elizabethan silver communion cup was cruelly melted down. His boxy high altar of 1865 is the only jarring note here, the details much too small and fussy for such a nobly exposed situation, and made all the more glaringly obvious by the proximity to the south of a severely simple Early English piscina. Happily, the beautiful plain octagonal traceried 15th-century font survives, its surface retooled but to good effect.

The east window has forceful glass of 1862 by Michael O'Connor (*1801-67*), and in the south aisle there is late Victorian glass by Kempe and Co. and four characteristically fine early 20th-century Arts and Crafts windows by Mary Lowndes (*1857-1929*). There are also two sturdy 17th-century wooden communion tables to look out for, one of which is somewhat battered and neglected. At the west end there are two small war memorial tablets commemorating the 19 local people killed in World War I, and the 13 killed in World War II.

The church contains several damaged late-medieval tomb-chests, but they don't amount to much. There is thus all the more reason to be grateful for the survival of the astonishing chantry chapel that fills an entire bay on the south side of the choir. This was added by the Ninth Baron, Thomas De La Warr (*died 1554*) in his lifetime, though he was not buried here since the Suppression of Chantries (*1547*) intervened.

The chantry chapel is the epitome of that particularly happy moment in the history of English decorative art when the native late-Gothic tradition was in imaginative dialogue with Renaissance motifs arriving indirectly from Italy via France and the Low Countries. Entered from the north-west, the chantry chapel has a solid canopy with cresting along the top supported on four corner columns with two tiers of reliefs showing shield-bearing angels and *putti*, with 12 substantial gabled niches which once held statues, the interiors of which have recently been distractingly painted Windsor blue. The columns are decorated with tiny plump cherubs amid vines, a Woodwose (or Wild Man of the Woods), standing men in armour and, on the north-east column, a delightful little genre scene of boys raiding an apple-tree and throwing fruit down to a girl who holds up her skirt to catch it. On another column Death as a skeleton reaches round to grasp a crowned woman, very much within the convention of the Dance of Death. The many spandrels house a variety of tiny lions, dragons, mermen, and so on. At ground level is a Gothic tomb-chest, and there is beautiful fan-vaulting inside with decorated suspended bosses. Look out for the delightful reredos on the east wall with its now empty niches and arabesques with tiny lute-bearing cherubs, masks, vases, and other Italianate motifs.

Often overlooked, the later monuments at Boxgrove are also of considerable interest. These include the nobly reticent standing monument on the east wall of the north transept commemorating Sir William Morley (*died 1701*), an MP and Lieutenant of the county. Set up in 1718, it is a late example of a type of monument popular with Restoration courtiers and featuring a large upright blazing urn standing on a tall plinth. Examples from the 1660s onwards can be found in Westminster Abbey, at Tonbridge and Hunton in Kent, at Willingdon in Sussex, and elsewhere.

Nearby on the north wall of the north transept is the particularly well-carved monument to Sir William Morley's daughter Mary, Countess of Derby (*died 1752*), with a panelled altar carrying a sloping-sided Grecian sarcophagus with a scrolly lid, in front of a tall mottled grey obelisk-shaped back-plate. On the front of the sarcophagus is an extremely fine relief showing the Countess seated under a tree distributing alms to a poor family, while reaching round to point towards Halnaker House in the background, the former seat of the De La Warr family. This is represented as a Palladian mansion, although the ruins only a mile or so from Boxgrove are of a once-substantial Tudor house. Her epitaph notes that 'Her Calmness And Patience In Adversity Were As Exemplary As Her / Humility And Moderation In Prosperity'.

It is probably by Thomas Carter the Younger who ran a busy yard supplying chimney-pieces for large houses and was employed by the Prince Regent at Carlton House around 1785. He also worked variously for Robert Adam, Henry Holland and Sir John Soane, and was responsible for the superb monument to Challoner Chute in the chapel at The Vyne in Hampshire, described by Rupert Gunnis as 'one of the noblest works of late eighteenth century sculpture in England'.[1]

---

1. *Rupert Gunnis, Dictionary of Britsh Sculptors 1660-1851, 1951, p. 86*

Getting there   National grid ref. SU908076
◉ Boxgrove is 4 miles (6 kilometres) north-east of Chichester, just off the A27. Easily accessible by local buses. ◉ Open daily. Details on Diocesan website: **www.diochi.org.uk**

ST BARTHOLOMEW

BRIGHTON

Towering above the ramshackle urban muddle at the south end of the London Road entrance to central Brighton, St Bartholomew is justly celebrated as one of the most important late Victorian churches in the country – not that it conforms to any familiar comparable standards. A vast red-brick barn of a building with the highest nave of any church in England, it was built between 1872 and 1874 by the Anglo-Catholic Fr. A. D. Wagner (*1824-1902*) who together with his father was responsible for several other local churches. At the time the mean-spirited local authority threatened to fine him 42 shillings for supposedly exceeding the agreed height by four feet. Given the remorseless and wholly unnecessary devastation of so much of historic inner Brighton by corrupt council fiat over the past 50 years, from the old market to the piers, one feels that little has changed.

Until recently there was a marvellous view of St Bartholomew from the train as one swept into Brighton station, but now, alas, the prospect is obscured by hideous new office blocks, and one needs to look across from the east side of the town to gauge its full architectural impact. Built like most late-Victorian High Church foundations to serve a predominantly working-class local congregation, it stares imperiously southwards towards the jolly late-Georgian pinnacled tower of Sir Charles Barry's church of St Peter (*1824-28*) at the top of the Old Steine, which seems to shrink away nervously from this imposingly majestic statement of evangelising populist Anglo-Catholic confidence in the face of Regency-Gothick gaiety. The local legend that it was built to the Biblical dimensions of Noah's Ark has no basis in fact but reflects its abiding local popularity, translated into rather delightfully fanciful folklore.

Designed by the little-known Edmund Scott (*1828-95*), the effect is strongly sculptural, and must have been even more astonishing before the fading of the diapered brickwork on the outside. A huge, severely plain rectangular basilica, the south end boasts an enormous rose window and four small lancets high above a statue of the patron saint in a canopied niche. Entering below this at the south door is an incredibly moving experience. One takes in the entire interior at once, the polychrome patterning of the brickwork much more apparent than it is outside. Everything is focused on what seems to be the east end (although it is actually the north, since the available site meant that the church is aligned north-south rather than east-west like most churches), with an appropriately plain timber roof resting on massive brick shafts and lost in shadows. Yet the interior is not dark, its volume defined by constantly changing diffused light from the nine tall clerestory windows on each side.

The north wall rises like a vast cliff of brick, with a huge ghostly white crucifix which is partly painted and partly incised on encaustic tiles. Below this stands an enormous aedicule, spectacularly faced with red and green marble, housing the high altar. Almost everything else below the crucifix was added between 1899 and 1908 to the design of the distinguished Arts and Crafts designer Henry Wilson (*1864-1924*), an assistant of the celebrated architect-designer John Dando Sedding (*1838-91*). All this is raised above the nave by four steps, on which stand Wilson's beautiful Art Nouveau brass altar rails with inset blue enamel medallions, and the two towering marble lamp-stands carrying flaming bronze urns which flank the high altar. The large glittering mosaics were designed by F. Hamilton Jackson in 1911, and the 1912 bronze altar crucifix is by McCulloch & Co. of Kennington.

Like Bentley's Westminster Cathedral, St Bartholomew is a great temple of neo-Byzantine taste, relieved throughout by Art Nouveau decoration of the highest order, including three superb silver hanging sanctuary lamps. To the left of the sanctuary is Wilson's pulpit, a larger and more ambitious version of the pulpit at Holy Trinity, Sloane Street in London, which is Sedding's masterpiece. It consists of a wide, sea-green panelled marble balcony raised high on mottled brown marble columns with a cream marble panelled apse behind, the whole thing surmounted by a huge suspended circular sounding-board. The pulpit is balanced at the west end by Wilson's matching baptistery, with a vast octagonal font of dark green marble edged with moulded copper, standing on three wide circular steps and set against a stunning screen of pale grey and pale green marble panels. The contrast with the surrounding acres of brickwork is dramatically effective, Byzantine in the tradition of the early churches of Rome, and of San Marco in Venice and the great marble-clad brick basilicas of the Venetian lagoon, including Santa Maria at Torcello and Santa Maria and San Donato at Murano.

Further down the long east wall stands Wilson's Lady Altar, with its magnificently glistening altar frontal of silver plate on copper showing the Adoration of the Magi surrounded by a rich array of raised circular bosses including Assyrian symbols of the planets paying homage with the Sun represented as a lion, Mars as a wolf, Jupiter as a thunderbolt, Mercury as a chained serpent, Venus as an owl, the Moon as a stag, and Saturn as a scorpion. Above this stands an astonishingly beautiful Art Nouveau silver crucifix which was originally made for the high altar and transferred here in 1912.

Back at the west end under the organ gallery is the chapel of the Holy Child, which by contrast is entirely English and late-Gothic in appearance, with a delightful carved and painted coved wooden canopy with a frieze of vine-scroll as if from the rood screen of a late medieval East Anglian or Devon church. Last but not least, look out for Wilson's free-standing octagonal red and green marble holy-water stoup at the south end of the nave, intended, like so much else here, as an enduring promise of a better life.

Getting there   National grid ref. TQ312051

❷ Ann Street, Brighton, is about ten minutes' walk west of Brighton station.

❷ Usually open. Check the Diocesan website: **www.diochi.org.uk**

ST NICHOLAS

BRIGHTON

Perched on a hilltop from which, for most of its history, it over-looked the little fishing port of Brighthelmstone far below on the shoreline of the once empty bay stretching from modern-day Kemp Town to Shoreham, the old parish church of Brighton was dedicated in 1260 to St Nicholas of Myra, the patron saint of sailors. During a voyage to the Holy Land from his native Turkey in the fourth century his prayers had calmed a storm at sea, and many coastal churches were dedicated to him, including St Nicholas at Old Shoreham. Like several other Sussex coastal parishes including Middleton, Atherington and Kingston-by-Ferring, the original settlement was consumed by the relentless forces of coastal erosion. Daniel Defoe reported in the 1720s that the sea

> is very unkind to this town, and has by its continual encroachments, so gain'd
> upon them, that in a little time more they might reasonably expect it would
> eat up the whole town, above 100 houses having been devoured by the water in
> a few years past.[1]

Replacing an earlier Norman church, the present low building shelters behind a squat, battlemented 14th-century west tower. Both the interior and exterior were, alas, thoroughly gone over by the

---

1. *op.cit., p.130*

Gothic-Revivalist architect Richard Cromwell Carpenter (*1812-55*) between 1852 and 1854, when all the Georgian fittings were unceremoniously flung out. Behind a much-restored late-medieval wooden screen the chancel is rather dark, not least because of the wholesale wall-paintings by the firm of Charles Eames Kempe to the design of the Brighton-born architect Somers Clark (*1841-1926*), with trailing foliage, angels and so on. In themselves these are rather good, but it's difficult to see them because of the unsympathetic re-glazing of all the windows in the church by Kempe between 1878 and 1897.

Much the most important thing at St Nicholas's is the magnificent drum-shaped lead-lined stone font (*c.1160*), which is all that survives from the original church. Although the surfaces were partly re-cut in 1745, little lasting harm seems to have been done. The style has no close parallel in England, which has led some to suggest that it was carved in France and imported, although there are no exact French parallels either. It illustrates a sequence of scenes, rather like a scroll. First comes The Last Supper with Christ seated at a draped table, one hand raised in blessing above a chalice, and flanked by six scowling, cowled apostles, three on each side. Then come two more hooded figures between columns before the next scene which includes a large sailing ship at sea and is thought to represent one of St Nicholas's miracles, when he saved some sailors from drowning by pouring holy oil onto the waves which ripple energetically under their boat. This is followed by the Baptism of Christ, with Jesus shown up to his waist in water flanked by two angels who obligingly hold out his robe and what appears to be a towel.

A band of chevron decoration runs round the top of the font, and there is a wide decorative frieze below the narrative scenes. This includes a type of scrolling foliage known as rinceau, with little trefoiled flowers and big leafy palmettes, and flowing zig-zag and patterned semi-circles filled with half-rosettes, which seem to have inspired the carver who was later responsible for two of the four sides of the font at St Mary de Haura, New Shoreham (*see p56*). Though largely covered in grey paint it is, on the whole, remarkably well preserved. Fortunately, it has long been removed from under a most elaborate towering carved stone font-cover-cum-Wellington Memorial designed by Carpenter and carved by John Birnie Philip in 1853, along the lines of the Eleanor Crosses which marked the overnight stops made by the funeral procession from Lincoln to London of Queen Eleanor of Castile in 1290. Now placed at the west end of the church, it bristles with crockets and buttresses and is as unmistakeably and endearingly Victorian as the Albert Memorial.

As one would expect, there are many small memorials dating back to the Regency period and reflecting the large numbers of people who came to Brighton for their health and entertainment. These include a nice tablet to Elizabeth Leigh (*died 1826*), with an inscription on a plain white altar on top of which is a small spray of well-carved flowers within which lurks a chrysalis from which a rather alarmingly large naturalistic butterfly is escaping. Who is this by? It is, sadly, rather grimy.

A larger upright white marble Grecian-style tablet by the distinguished sculptor Sir Richard Westmacott (*1775-1856*) commemorates Frances Crosbie Fairfield (*died 1830*), with an angel helping lift her up towards a radiant sunburst above, an image he borrowed from the sculptor John Flaxman. The inscription underneath is flanked by two severely plain amphorae.

However, the best monument, again by Sir Richard Westmacott, is to his wife, Lady Westmacott, who died in 1834. This consists of an extremely Roman-looking matronly bust, with a cloak falling behind her shoulders from the back of her head. The brief inscription describes the maker as 'Maritus Infelix' (Her Unhappy Husband).

The surrounding churchyard has, alas, been landscaped, with many weathered gravestones lined up along the inside of the perimeter walls, and a few good sarcophagi railed in for safe-keeping, including the striking tomb of Amon Wilds (*1762-1833*), the architect (with his partner Charles Busby) of much of Regency Brighton. It is thought that his son, Amon Henry Wilds, designed the shell-covered tomb. Near the north door there is still an excellent headstone set up by order of George IV commemorating Phoebe Hessel (*died 1821*) whom it explains 'served for many years as a private Soldier in the 5th Regt of Foot'. Born in Stepney in 1713, Hessel enlisted in the army as a man in order to be with her lover. She fought at the Battle of Fontenoy in 1745 under the command of the Duke of Cumberland, and died in Brighton at the astonishing age of 108. George IV had granted her a pension, and it was he who commissioned her gravestone.

An adjacent stone marks the burial place of the redoubtable Martha Gunn who died in 1815 aged 77. Befriended by the Prince-Regent, she was the most celebrated of Brighton's female 'dippers', and for more than 60 years assisted visiting lady bathers in and out of the sea. Her 1796 portrait by John Russell hangs in the tea-room of the Royal Pavilion, and her house still stands at 36 East Street. The gravestone also records the death of her husband Stephen and their son, the unforgettably named Friend Gunn, who died in 1784 aged 22. Both stones owe their survival to tall protective railings.

Getting there   National grid ref. TQ307045
- St Nicholas is about ten minutes' walk due south of Brighton station, near the Clock Tower at the bottom of Dyke Road.
- Rarely open. For visiting arrangements check with The Revd. R. Chavner tel. 01273 709045.
- Details on Diocesan website: **www.diochi.org.uk**

COOMBES CHURCH

COOMBES

Set well back on a shelf scooped out high up on the chalky slope of the Downs above Shoreham, with a protective screen of trees behind, Coombes church stands in a small walled churchyard surrounded by upland fields with working farm buildings to the south. A handful of cottages a little way down the hillside marks an ancient settlement which stretches back at least to Saxon times. Happily, Coombes was remote enough to escape the 'improving' intentions of Victorian restorers, and thus remains quietly eloquent of centuries of accumulated local rural piety. From *c.*1515 to 1786 the former manor-house at nearby Applesham was in the hands of the Shelley family, which held much farm-land in these parts. The church's original dedication has not survived, but this only adds to the singularity of the place. As a local parishioner told me, she feels she is not so much a member of the Church of England as of the Church of Coombes.

First recorded in 1086, it is a simple two-cell flint building with a plain early Norman nave and chancel arch giving on to a chancel of about 1200. The chancel windows are late medieval while the small three-light east window is 16th century. The remains of former doors and windows can be seen throughout the church. The line of the roof is interrupted only by a bell-cote at the west end. A former west tower is shown on an estate plan of 1677, but it fell in 1724, taking with it the extreme west end of the nave. The present west wall and arched window must have been set up shortly afterwards. To the north of the altar stands a severely plain early medieval jointed chest, made of big boards seated in grooved corner-supports known as 'stiles', the joints fixed by wooden dowel-pegs. It has been patched up over the years, and may in part date back to the 13th century.

Like the door through which one enters, the single bell is seemingly even older, and of the 12th century, making it one of the oldest in the country. It has sounded the religious year across the surrounding fields and woods and farms for almost 900 years. The font is a wide shallow lead-lined circular bowl, as plain as a millstone, and stands on a plain square brick plinth. It could be of the tenth or the 20th centuries, which suggests much about the continuity of font design in rural Sussex. The floor is patched throughout with brick and worn glazed medieval tiles, to delight-fully homely effect.

In 1949 the remains of an important sequence of early 12th-century wall-paintings were discovered, from the same Sussex school as those at Clayton and Hardham, and like them, damaged. The prevailing style is immensely animated, and with their long, sad, harrowed faces and great decorative confidence, the figures at Coombes may instructively be compared to contemporary illuminated manuscripts from St Albans, and the two magnificent carved stone panels preserved in Chichester Cathedral. Given that so few early Romanesque English wall-paintings survive, these moving fragments, probably painted by an itinerant work-shop, suggest volumes about the scale and quality of what we have lost elsewhere.

Above the 16th-century south porch there is a Visitation scene and frag-ments of the story of the Nativity continue along the north wall. The faded remains of Christ in Majesty in an oval mandorla are on the chancel arch, surrounded by the symbols of the four Evangelists, of which the splendid winged red lion of St Mark is much the best preserved. On the north side of the chancel arch are further substantial remains of a scene showing Christ seated on a throne delivering the keys to Saint Peter and a book to Saint Paul. The inner arch is decorated with a beautiful undu-lating pattern, perhaps in imitation of mosaic work, while the arch is held up on the north side by a lively little crouching painted caryatid, his mouth wide open from the strain. The corresponding figure on the south side has unfortunately not survived. They probably derived from contemporary carved stone prototypes of the kind found holding up a door lintel on the south side of the nave of Osimo Cathedral in Italy.

Elsewhere there is much simple imitation stonework, with the ghostly remains of a late 13th- or early 14th-century Annunciation which formerly flanked the east window, although there is no longer any trace of the Angel Gabriel on the north side. The prevailing colours throughout are pale green, cream, deep red and ochre. The imposts of the chancel arch are carved with small heads of uncertain date.

On the north wall of the nave are two small early 19th-century white marble tablets commemorating members of the Wyatt family, several generations of whom farmed hereabouts, and whose burial vault is marked by a slab on the floor. Above the blocked 15th-century doorway to a former vestry on the north side of the chancel is a plain Victorian marble tablet to members of the Gell family, and on the floor there are several late 17th- and early 18th-century slabs commemorating members of the Manning family. The latest of these, to John Manning (*died 1707*) and his wife Joanna (*died 1700*), has a well-carved circular achievement of arms at the top. On the east side of the altar rails is a badly worn 13th-century slab with traces of an incised cross, and two 18th-century slabs commemorating members of the Ingram family.

Reached at the end of a long winding lane, Coombes is a church to revisit at different seasons: in the winter snow, or at lambing time when the churchyard is clumped with snowdrops and early daffodils and the nearby farm buildings bustle with activity, or in high summer when plump contented sheep graze the fields. Sheltered in its little hollow and looking out across the wide horizons of the Adur valley, its atmosphere is always peaceful and serenely welcoming. Holy ground indeed.

Getting there   National grid ref. TQ191081

❯ Coombes is 2 miles (3 kilometres) north of the A27 between Lancing and New Shoreham.

❯ Open daily. If closed, the key is held at nearby Church Cottage.

❯ Details on the website: **www.coombes.co.uk**

HOLY TRINITY

CUCKFIELD

First mentioned in a Charter of 1092, the parish church of Holy Trinity at Cuckfield in north-east Sussex was steadily enlarged over the centuries in line with the growing prosperity of the compact hilltop market-town it serves. A south aisle and chapel were added in the 13th century, when the west tower was begun. The north aisle and chancel flanked by chapels were added in the 14th century, when the mighty buttressed and battlemented tower was completed, and the nave and chancel roofs were raised to allow the insertion of clerestory windows. A century later, these were shut off from the light when the aisle walls were raised to permit the construction of the dramatic sweeping roof one sees today. Another small chapel was added at the north-east end in the 16th century but was converted into a vestry in 1888 following decades of remorseless restoration work, starting under George Frederick Bodley (*1827-1907*) between 1855 and 1856, all of which contributed to the predominantly Victorian atmosphere inside.

Sadly all the old pews and the splendid 17th-century wooden triple-decker pulpit were thrown out at this time, but mercifully the unusual 13th-century font was spared, although heavily restored in 1846. The only real gain was the delightful south porch rebuilt in 1883 to the design of Bodley's pupil Charles Eames Kempe (*1837-1907*) who lived locally. He was also responsible for the picturesque 1887 lychgate through which one enters the churchyard. The entire roof was resurfaced with Horsham stone in the 1920s, to great effect, and the elegant broach-spire was replaced after a fire in 1980. This type of spire, typical of Sussex, consists of an octagonal pyramid rising from a square base, and gives a nice sense of uplift in contrast to the rather crushing effect of plain four-sided spires found at Rodmell and elsewhere. Fortunately the internal structure of the vast 15th-century roof was left alone. It consists of plastered panels with bosses at the connecting corners which contain many religious emblems and heraldic devices.

All this was rather charmingly painted in 1865 to Kempe's designs, and ten delightful very Pre-Raphaelite-looking carved wooden angels were added a year later high up on both sides of the nave beneath the hammer-beams which hold the roof together. The aisles were given plaster ceilings in 1801 having formerly been open to the rafters above, but all this was, alas, covered up with wooden ceilings by Kempe in 1899. The windows are 19th-century replacements. Even the main east window was reduced in height, all of which makes for a certain monotony to the interior, now condemned to perpetual gloom.

The history of Cuckfield and its inhabitants is more accurately reflected in the fascinating sequence of surviving monuments inside the church than by its architecture. The earliest of these is a group of 16th-century brasses, including one to Henry Bowyer (*died 1588*) on the floor of the south chapel. He is also commemorated together with his wife Elizabeth and their five children in a second, larger, framed brass plate. No less than 13 different monuments record members of the Burrell family, who were originally successful local masters of the Wealden iron-smelting trade. The earliest of these is a framed brass plate to Ninian Burrell (*died 1614*) and his widow who lived on until 1656, and their children. Their son Ninian (*died 1628*) is commemorated in the south chapel by a hanging marble wall-monument which follows the fashions of contemporary court taste. Made in London and laboriously transported in wagons for reassembly *in situ*, it shows him kneeling at a prayer-desk framed by big curtains that are being pulled back by two standing angels.

The Burrell monuments make for an instructive sequence illustrating the slowly changing history of English sculpture, continuing well into the 19th century. The best of these commemorates Captain Percy Burrell of the 6th regiment of the Dragoon Guards who was killed in action outside Buenos Aires on his 28th birthday in 1810. Carved by John Bacon Jr. it is a superb white marble hanging wall-monument at the west end of the south aisle and depicts the captain falling back into the arms of a fellow soldier. Not large, it is every bit as good as anything of the period in St Paul's Cathedral.

Much the most fascinating object in the church however is the tablet on the south wall of the north chapel commemorating Guy Carleton who died in 1628, and the two young children of his sister Anne who was married to the Vicar of Cuckfield. Guy and Anne's father, George Carleton, had been Vicar of Mayfield from 1589 to 1605, and was subsequently Bishop of Chichester from 1619 until his death in 1628.

Partly hidden by a chest, the monument consists of a beautifully incised slate plate bristling with astonishing emblems and mysterious accompanying texts, set in a carved freestone frame. The central epitaph lies inside a big incised heart, with emblems at each corner and on both sides. Above the epitaph is a demi-angel pointing to his heart with his left hand and to the top right emblem with his right hand. At the top left is an emblem showing an open eye inside a heart in a circular frame with Greek text, and at the top right is a smouldering heart resting on a book in a circular frame. At the bottom left is a superbly drawn emblem showing a seated cherub with a skull framed by a snake devouring its tail, an ancient symbol of immortality much used in the early 19th century by Sir John Soane. The image is closely related to emblem number 45 in George Wither's *A Collection Of Emblemes Ancient And Modern* (London, 1635).

At the lower right is an emblem depicting a skull resting on an hourglass with sprays of wheat coming out of its eyes. This is also strikingly similar to Wither's emblem number 21. On the left of the plate is a snake coiled round a tau-cross which again is very similar to Wither's emblem number 67. Finally, on the right is a downwards pointing arrow with the words 'Crux Christi Anchor Spei' (The Cross of Christ, Anchor of Hope). Does the monument pre-date Wither's book, and if so, did the Carleton family know him? One would like to know more about them and the history of this remarkable monument.

There are many other extremely rewarding things to look out for at Cuckfield, including a terrific large standing monument on the north side of the sanctuary dedicated to Charles Sergison, who died in 1732 at the great age of 78, having been Commissioner of the Navy from 1671 to 1712. By the distinguished early Georgian sculptor Thomas Adye, (died 1753), this consists of a pale grey marble altar carrying a dark grey sarcophagus on which rests the beautifully carved seated figure of Truth holding up a mirror in her right hand and an upright oval portrait medallion with her left hand, which is steadied by an engaging *putto* seated on the right. Last but by no means least, look out for the splendid 17th-century-style monument with its standing figures of three brothers killed in action in World War I, which is unfortunately hidden away high up under the tower.

Getting there   National grid ref. TQ303244

◈ Holy Trinty is on the B2036, north of the A272. Nearest train station is Haywards Heath, then a bus or bike-ride of about 4 miles (6 kilometres).

◈ Open daily. Check with the church office tel. 01444 456461.

◈ Details on the website: **www.cuckfieldholytrinity.co.uk**

ST SAVIOUR

EASTBOURNE

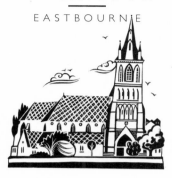

The dramatic population growth of many Victorian seaside resorts was widely reflected in new buildings, including railway-stations, hotels and churches. George Edmund Street's Eastbourne church of St Saviour (*1867-8*) reflected the shift of economic gravity away from the old inland town-centre with its ancient Norman parish church of St Mary, to the recently developed residential seafront district. Like William Butterfield's similarly imposing church of All Saints at Babbacombe (*1867*), John Dando Sedding's St Clement's at Bournemouth (*1873*), and many other examples around the country, the seaside environment encouraged particularly grand expressions of Victorian High Church values. On land given by the Duke of Devonshire, St Saviour reflects the widespread influence of the Oxford Movement within the Church of England and its associated revival of ritual and ceremony, requiring appropriately sumptuous fittings and furnishings.

G. E. Street (*1824-81*) had trained under the architect George Gilbert Scott (*1811-78*), through whom he became immersed in the values of the Gothic Revival, and especially the architecture of the 13th century. A devout High Church Anglican, Street designed his churches also to reflect his interest in Italian medieval brick architecture, and his offices served as the training ground for many of the next generation of young architects and designers responsible for the Arts and Crafts movement, including William Morris, Philip Webb, Richard Norman Shaw and

Sedding. In many respects St Saviour resembles the huge friary churches of Tuscany as much as any surviving Gothic building in England, with the telling addition of a dynamic tower at the north-west corner. This has richly diapered brickwork above the entrance, and is crowned by an elegant broach-spire.

Entering from the north via a vaulted stone porch under the tower, one quickly takes in the sheer size of the interior with its huge aisled nave under a high wooden wagon-roof. Everything is focused on the raised vaulted apsidal east end, seen beyond the splendidly decorated chancel arch. Above the arch is an immense roundel containing the image of Christ in Majesty surrounded by angels and the symbols of the four evangelists, painted directly onto the underlying brick, to terrific effect. The nave arcades are angled inwards on either side of the chancel, rising in two big concave pointed vaults lined with tiers of standing saints which flank the central scene.

The paintings are the work of Clayton and Bell, the successful company founded in 1857 by John Richard Clayton (*1827-1913*) and Alfred Bell (*1832-95*) who had both worked as draughtsmen for George Gilbert Scott. Initially concentrating on the design and manufacture of stained glass, they subsequently branched out into wall-paintings and mosaics. They were responsible for the design of the many mosaics lining the aisle walls here, which were made by the Salviati company of Venice, who made most of the company's mosaics including Clayton's extensive work for the Albert Memorial. It seems rather a shame that the 14 small Stations of The Cross from 1928 are hung in such a way as to interfere with the overall decorative scheme.

The walls of the chancel are richly clad with tiles and marble and elaborately gabled stone seating designed by Street and house more splendid smaller mosaics and wall paintings of angels and seated saints by Clayton and Bell, culminating in the carved and painted reredos of 1937 designed by W. H. Randolph Blacking. Note the beautiful carved wooden gallery on the south side of the choir, and the stunning wrought-iron screen to the chapel of St Peter on the north side. A baptistery was added at the west end in 1896, with mosaics on either side showing

St Augustine's mission to reconvert the English on the south wall, and on the north wall the seventh-century Christian Northumbrian king St Oswald, shown raising a wooden Cross after the battle of Heavenfield near Hexham in AD 635. It houses a big plain octagonal onyx font designed by Street, with a tall wooden pyramidical font-cover.

Clayton and Bell provided decorations for many such High Church interiors including St Peter's at Vauxhall (*1863-4*) built by the distinguished Victorian architect, John Loughborough Pearson, and the firm remained in business until the 1980s. Most of their glass at St Saviour was blown out during World War II, though some figures which survived can now be seen in the chapel of the Blessed Sacrament, on the south side of the nave. This was added in 1903 in memory of the church's founder and first vicar, the Reverend Henry Robert Whelpton (*1833-1902*). His tomb on the north side of the chapel has a large brass on top of a plain tomb-chest under a richly cusped and panelled arch. The splendid oak relief of the Burial of Christ on the altar was designed by George Jack (*1855-1931*), one of the leading woodcarvers of the Arts and Crafts movement.[1]

Happily the destroyed glass was more than matched by the splendid postwar replacements at the east end by Christopher Rahere Webb (*1886-1966*). Articled to the ecclesiastical designer Sir Ninian Comper, C.R. Webb was perhaps the best of all the of the designers who reacted against the darkness of so much late Victorian stained glass.[2] A superb draftsman, he was also extremely prolific in a career which lasted from the 1920s to the 1960s. He was responsible for superb replacement windows at Bristol, Chichester, Exeter and Southwark cathedrals.

Following the closure of the nearby church of St Peter in 1971, the two parishes were amalgamated. All the work by Clayton and Bell was superbly restored in the early 1990s.

1. *Amy Gaimster, George Jack, 1855-1931, Architect and Designer-Craftsman, William Morris Gallery, London, 2006.*
2. *Eileen Roberts, Christopher Webb and the Orchard House Studio, the Journal of Stained Glass, Vol. XXV, 2001, pp. 79-96.*

Getting there   National grid ref. TV610987
❯ St Saviour is on South Street, central Eastbourne, about ten minutes' walk from the station.
❯ Open daily 08.30-15.00. Details on the website: **http://myweb.tiscali.co.uk/saviours/**

ST MARY THE VIRGIN

GLYNDE

Set slightly athwart the foundations of the medieval church which it replaced, St Mary the Virgin at Glynde enjoys a superb commanding view across the Ouse valley. Built between 1763 and 1765 by Richard Trevor, Bishop of Durham and owner of Glynde Place immediately to the north, it is the only Palladian village church in Sussex and its uncompromising Neo-Classicism is emblematic of the 'reasonable Christianity' of the 18th century. Designed by Sir Thomas Robinson, who was also responsible for the rebuilding of his own family seat at Rokeby in Yorkshire, St Mary is a plain rectangular building with a west porch flanked by two big blank arched niches. Built of Portland stone and knapped flints by John Morris and William Langridge of Lewes, it has an open bell-cote on top of the west end housing a bell of 1619 above a grandly swaggering heraldic escutcheon on the front of the pediment. Ten years later Robinson used much the same design for a new church at Rokeby which was, alas, later comprehensively altered by Victorian modifications.

Bishop Trevor was a pioneering adversary of anti-semitism and a great patron of the arts who, besides remodelling the Great Hall of the adjacent family seat at Glynde Place, had employed Robinson to design the immensely likeable 1760 gatehouse to the ancient palace of the Bishops of Durham at Bishop Auckland in County Durham. He was also a notable ecclesiastical benefactor and was responsible for, amongst other things, the gift of a magnificent sequence of paintings depicting Jacob and his sons by the great 17th-century Spanish artist Francesco de Zurbarán (*1598-1664*). Happily, these works still grace the palace walls at Bishop Auckland, in spite of misguided attempts in 2001 by the Church Commissioners to sell them off, an unpopular move that was fortunately prevented but only as the result of a strenuous campaign of local and national opposition.

The original glass in the arched Venetian east window at Glynde was by William Peckitt of York and incorporated many Flemish 16th-century roundels and other painted panels which were subsquently reset within later windows when the church was completely re-glazed by the firm of Charles Eames Kempe from 1894 to 1916. Their cloyingly vapid late-Victorian religious scenes are all the worse for being framed in strikingly unsuitable pseudo-High Renaissance borders. The predominantly golden-toned pieces of old Flemish glass are delightful, and in themselves Kempe's borders are rather good, but their combination with the unusually feeble central scenes is memorably horrible and an object lesson in how not to do it. A large, obtrusive walnut screen was set up at the east end in 1895, but fortunately was removed in 1983. One only wishes that the Kempe windows could be similarly treated.

The walls throughout are covered with richly decorated hessian, rather like a ballroom, and there is much fine plasterwork around the east window and on the ceiling. All of this is charmingly of its time but struck most Victorians as intolerably secular. Reached by a nice staircase, the west gallery was added in 1841. On the front is a splendid carved wooden cartouche of the Arma Christi with the instruments used in the torture and death of Christ depicted around a central cross, a rare subject in English churches after the Middle Ages. It is set in a pierced strapwork frame surmounted by a finely carved pelican in her piety, symbolising the Christ's self-sacrifice. Underneath the gallery is a stylish 18th century white marble baluster-shaped font.

There are no monuments inside the church at Glynde save for a cluster of ledger-stones and small brass plaques to members of the Morley and Trevor families on the floor of the railed-off Sanctuary.

In front of the church the sharply downward-sloping rectangular churchyard is well stocked with sturdy Victorian gravestones, which make a good group together with a stone war memorial like an ancient churchyard cross with a beautifully carved Crucifixion in a small gabled niche on top. To the east the churchyard has been landscaped and the older gravestones lined up along the north wall. Standing in splendid isolation is a square monument to John Hewes (*died 1750*) with a big blazing urn on top. There is also an excellent freestanding sarcophagus on the south side of the church to Mrs Eliza Ellman who died in 1790.

She was the wife of John Ellman the celebrated breeder of the prize-winning Southdown sheep, whose local farm was visited by George III among other leading figures of the day. He retired in 1829 having been presented with a silver cup in gratitude for his work by the land-owners of Sussex, and a silver vase in 1805 by the Duke of Bedford, as well as the Board of Agriculture's gold medal in 1819 for the best cultivated farm in Sussex. His celebrated fairness to his employees did not prevent his being attacked by the ever-combative reformer William Cobbett.

Against the wall are many carved gravestones worth looking out for, including the memorial to Thomas Howell (*died 1765*) in the style of an earlier age with a nice winged hourglass at the top. The Reverend Thomas Davies (*died 1789*) is commemorated by a stone with a small relief of a mourning angel holding up a portrait medallion, like a miniature version of a much grander contemporary monument, while his wife Mary's monument has a small seated angel holding an anchor symbolising hope. Another contemporary gravestone to William Als has a splendid small circular relief of Father Time holding out his scythe and an hourglass. The spirit of a later age is already reflected in an 1811 headstone with an unusual and delightful small inset oval terracotta still-life of pomegranates and other fruit in a basket. This is by the Heathfield stonemason Jonathan Harmer (*1762-1839*).

Getting there   National grid ref. TQ456092

◉ St Mary the Virgin is half a mile (800 metres) north of the A27 on the Glynde road between Lewes and Eastbourne, or ten minutes north of Glynde station.

◉ Open daily. Details on Diocesan website: **www.diochi.org.uk**

ST MARY THE VIRGIN

HORSHAM

The market town of Horsham was long famous for the manufacture of iron horseshoes and bolts for cross-bows as well as the beautiful local grey-brown stone which was formerly widely used to great effect for roofing throughout West Sussex. The town centre was cruelly vandalised in the late 20th century, leaving little of architectural cohesion or value apart from The Causeway, a long, wide, tree-lined street which includes the excellent local museum, housed in a substantial gabled late-Elizabethan half-timbered town-house. Stretching south towards the surrounding countryside and the Arun, The Causeway leads directly to the ancient parish church of St Mary The Virgin.

The north-west corner of the nave survives from the early 12th century, as well as the base of the present west tower with its simple late Norman arched sandstone doorway. There was extensive rebuilding in the early 13th century reflecting the town's growing prosperity, as is immediately apparent outside from the elegant shingled broach-spire, and inside from the cool stately five-bay aisled nave with its severely plain round piers, giving directly onto the late 13th-century three-bay chancel, with octagonal piers. There is no intervening chancel arch. It's well worth training one's binoculars on the external corbel-table high up on the tower where many excellent carved stone heads are located. A re-used early 12th-century carved stone head stares ferociously down the nave from the apex of the later tower arch, some feet below the small painted Hanoverian Royal Arms which are hung inexplicably high. The badly battered octagonal late medieval font survives in the nave, revealing the cruel effects of Puritan vandalism and many years of weathering out of doors at some time in its history. The former rood screen of 1522 survived until 1825, and the loss of the strong horizontal note it must have provided contributes to the sense of unrelieved internal emptiness.

Leading local families added chantry chapels to the north and south aisles in the early 14th and mid-15th centuries respectively, the latter boasting a splendid timber roof bristling with painted Tudor roses and heraldic shields. The main east window is a spectacular affair of seven lights, an 1865 replica of the 15th-century original, with typically forceful glass by the O'Connors. This was also the date of extensive and rather brutal internal restoration by Samuel Sanders Teulon (*1812-73*), compensated by his picturesque, oddly Dutch-looking gabled south aisle. A rarity in Sussex, there is some exceptionally good late Victorian glass by Heaton, Butler & Bayne in the west windows of both aisles, and elsewhere. It is also worth looking out for the 1924 stained glass figure of Christ in the Trinity chapel, designed by Frederick Etchells (*1886-1973*) who was a veteran of Roger Fry's Omega Workshops and responsible for fine modern church fittings at West Dean and elsewhere.

The large churchyard sloping down towards the river contains several grand 18th-century stone sarcophagi, and many well-carved Georgian and early Victorian gravestones, most of which have been herded together close to the church. These include fine memorials to Mrs Mary Jones (*died 1759*) with two jolly winged cherub-heads flanked by two ferocious skulls in profile, and to Charity Young (*died 1797*). Others include beefy little trumpeting angels, and there are several with small engagingly carved scenes including one to Sarah Sillyard (*died 1787*) which shows a plump little angel hovering with a crown held out above a book, while another to Thomas Griffith (*died 1796*) depicts a woman leaning in mourning by a wide draped urn on a plinth. These are all from a local masons' yard, which was evidently responsible for several tablets in the church which show clearly how such headstones would have looked when new.

Inside the church the sequence of surviving monuments begins with the rather routine memorial to Sir Thomas de Braose (*died 1395*) with a damaged recumbent freestone effigy which is much less engaging than the small jolly brass in the south chancel aisle commemorating an un-named lady of a century later. On the north side of the sanctuary is the free-standing canopied monument to Thomas Hoo (*died 1485*). This contains a delicate fan-vault, with two small carved angels on the west end of the canopy, and another angel playing a lute on the south side.

Much the most attractive surviving monument at Horsham however is to Mrs Elisabeth Delves who died in childbirth in 1654 at the age of 25. Dating from a period of widespread economic and social collapse, when few monuments were produced, it is by the leading London mason-sculptor Edward Marshall (*1598-1675*) who was appointed Master Mason to the Crown in 1660. Like his earlier monument to Lady Culpepper (*1638*) at Hollingbourne in Kent, it consists of a finely carved marble tomb-chest with a moulded black lid supporting a recumbent white marble figure. The effigy is very stylish in the streamlined style characteristic of Marshall. She lies with her eyes open and her right hand resting on her chest, the surfaces highly polished as Marshall and his clients evidently liked. An endearingly doggy lion reclines at her feet, still as entirely a creature of heraldry as the lions on the early 14th-century monuments on the south side of Winchelsea church.

On the front of the tomb-chest is a large inscription panel with luxuriantly carved heraldic escutcheons at either end which retain traces of original polychrome decoration. The Delves monument may also instructively be compared to Marshall's 1655 tomb for Mrs Mary Audley at Sanderstead in Surrey. Like much of Marshall's best work it follows the restrained courtly type established by Nicholas Stone's 1631 Westminster Abbey monument to Sir George Villiers and his wife. Unfortunately, a recent wooden altar rail rather obscures one's view of it, which is regrettable since it is much the finest work of art in Horsham and one of the best monuments in the county.

There are also many interesting later tablets, most of which were unfortunately rounded up and hidden away under the tower in the course of 19th-century restoration work. These include a typically simple oval Regency tablet to John Medwyn who died in a fall from a tree aged 21 in 1806, and a small hanging wall-monument to Captain Richard Marriott of the East India Company, who died 'of a painful and lingering disorder' at the age of 28 in 1805. This also shows his stricken widow kneeling by an urn.

Another severely plain but rather grimy Regency epitaph on the south side of the west door commemorates Sir Bysshe Shelley (*died 1815*), the builder of the fabulously eccentric Castle Goring near Worthing, which is Gothick at the front and Palladian at the back. It also commemorates his first wife, whose father had been Vicar of Horsham, and their daughter Mary. Sir Bysshe's MP son Timothy is commemorated on the north side of the door. Different branches of this old Sussex family, whose funeral vault lies under the south chapel, had homes in Lewes, Michelgrove, Worminghurst, and at Field Place near Horsham, where Sir Bysshe's grandson Percy Bysshe Shelley, the great Romantic poet, was born in 1792. He is also remembered here by a small white marble tablet adjacent to the vault, although his ashes are interred in Rome and his heart at Christchurch Priory in Hampshire. The local museum (Horsham Museum on The Causeway) is rich in Shelley memorabilia.

Getting there   National grid ref. TQ170302

- St Mary the Virgin is on The Causeway in central Horsham.
- Horsham train station is on the London to Chichester line.
- Open daily 10.00-16.00. Details on website: **www.horshamchurches.co.uk/st_mary.htm**

ST ANDREW

HOVE

I n spite of later changes, it is not too difficult to imagine Brunswick Square and its accompanying seafront Terrace as they appeared when first built in the mid-1820s, looking out directly onto open country-side to the north, and along the undeveloped beach to the west. Initially known as Brunswick Town, the square was the centrepiece of a grand speculative development designed to terminate the west end of the Brighton esplanade, balancing the slightly earlier grandeur of Kemp Town at the eastern end. Described in 1835 as 'most incontestably the handsomest spot in Brighton,'[1] the Brunswick development included a library, baths and its own market, all intended to serve the prosperous incoming population. From 1835 to 1872 the town's main cricket ground lay immediately to the west. A new chapel was also built at the seaside end of the adjacent Waterloo Street.

Dedicated to St Andrew, it opened in July 1828 and was immedi-ately popular with its socially exclusive congregation, the members of which were required to pay substantial box-pew fees, and entered by three separate doors at the west end to preserve social hierarchies.[2] It was designed by the young Charles Barry (*1795-1860*) who had already built St Peter's church in central Brighton, and is best known for the later rebuilding of the Houses of Parliament with Augustus Welby Pugin

1. John Bruce, *the History of Brighton with the Latest Improvements*, 1835.
2. John Vigar & Mike Robins, *St Andrew's Church, Waterloo Street, Hove*, 2005.

(*1812-52*). The chapel has a handsome classical west front of stucco and Portland stone with a central arched entrance with a band of guilloche decoration flanked by paired Corinthian pilasters and two blank arched recesses, which are perhaps an homage to the west front of St Mary at Glynde. It is capped by a small charming bell-tower. A narrow vestibule provides stairs to the west gallery.

The fine church we see today is in fact of three distinct periods. Originally a plain, broad, aisle-less rectangle filled by tall box-pews with arched classical side windows, the chapel was substantially enlarged in 1882 by Barry's son Charles Barry Junior, who added a new apsidal sanctuary and flanking chapels at the east end on the site of a former stable. This was accomplished by creating a big chancel arch in the middle of the former east wall, flanked by Ionic columns, with smaller arches on either side, leading to a vestry in the north-east corner and a small Lady Chapel to the south. He also inserted a shallow dome above the altar behind the new chancel arch, with a shallow panelled apse behind it.

At the same time the rest of the building was largely refurbished inside. Additions included the present open nave seating and the choir furnishings including stalls and the splendid neo-Jacobean pulpit with its delightful sounding-board above. The west gallery was rebuilt and a large Restoration-style organ-case was added on the north side of the sanctuary with finely carved falls of flowers in the Wren manner. Skylights at both ends provide a very Italianate effect of top-lighting, and this combined with the use of arches and the saucer-dome, together with classical brackets with winged cherub-heads below the nave windows and at the west end, creates a distinctly Soanian sense of spatial ambiguity and complexity.

In 1922 Fr. Stanley Kirkley became rector and began a long-term process of redecoration, bringing the church more in line with Brighton's mainly High Church tastes. He added a large classical pedimented aedicule above the altar and a corresponding baldacchino with four fluted Corinthian columns above the white marble Georgian pedestal-font that stands in its own small handsome frame at the west end. The Queen Anne-style circular wooden font-cover was designed by Randolph

Blacking in the 1920s, and is decorated with the ancient Greek decorative motif of alternating anthemion (honeysuckle) and palmettes, so characteristic of both the 18th-century, and mid-Victorian Greek-Revival taste. Blacking also designed the bronze altar rails at the east end, which were originally surmounted by eight cherub-heads, seven of which were sadly stolen by squatters during the 1990s.

In the 1920s Fr. Kirkley also decorated the shallow dome above the high altar with a central sun-burst against an azure night sky with stars, a shooting-star, the planet Saturn, and a crescent moon, all visible only from below in the sanctuary. In its way, it is a sister-image to Karl Friedrich Schinkel's magical 1815 design of a crescent moon rising against rows of shimmering stars which he used for the entrance of the Queen of the Night in Mozart's *The Magic Flute*, an opera which so perfectly embodies the enlightening sprit of the Age of Reason. It is a lovely image, and seems highly appropriate in this essentially Georgian-feeling church, re-imagined in Art Deco style.

The unobtrusive Victorian glass, mainly with standing saints, is by Hardman of Birmingham, the best of which is the grey and golden-toned grisaille rose-window with St Richard of Chichester and other saints at the north end of the east wall, although sadly this is largely hidden behind the organ-case. The small semi-circular window high up behind the main altar is also very good. In the south-east corner are two excellent early windows by Christopher Rahere Webb (*1886-1966*) who frequently worked with Blacking, and by whom equally good later work can be seen in Sussex at St Saviour in Eastbourne (*see p.42*), St Mary in Willingdon (*see p.76*) and St Wilfrid, Church Norton. At the east end of the Lady Chapel is his beautiful Annunciation commemorating Oliver Scott (*1927*), and above the arched entrance to the chapel is an equally good rose-window (*1938*) with the Christ-child flanked by the Three Magi and Shepherds.

By the end of the 19th century there were many memorial tablets on the nave walls, but Fr. Kirkley removed most of these to the west end vestibule, leaving only four inside the main body of the church, together with four small brass plates commemorating servicemen killed in World War I. The two best tablets in the nave are in similar Grecian-style and commemorate Lord Charles Henry Somerset (*died 1831*) with a robed woman holding out a wreath towards a vase on a plinth, and Sir George Dallas Bt. (*died 1833*), with a robed woman seated mourning, head in hand, by a Grecian gravestone, a nice example of a monument-within-a-monument. The church was declared redundant in 1990 and after various travails passed into the care of the Churches Conservation Trust. There is an active local Friends' Group.

Getting there   National grid ref. TQ299043

⊚ St Andrew is just off the seafront at the bottom of Waterloo Street, south of Western Road.

⊚ Buses run from Brighton station, or it is about 25 minutes' walk. The building is in the care of The Churches Conservation Trust.

⊚ Open Sunday afternoons 14.00-16.00. Details on the website: **www.visitchurches.org.uk**

ST MARY DE HAURA

NEW SHOREHAM

By the late 11th century the Adur was already silting up, thus preventing access to the established Saxon port of Old Shoreham, and around the year 1100 a new town was begun a couple of miles downstream at New Shoreham, though this did not prevent the Normans from extensively remodelling the Saxon church at Old Shoreham. This work was undertaken by the de Braose family, who were based at Bramber Castle which defended the entrance to what was then the wide river-mouth of the Adur, and protected the port of Steyning further upstream. Their further decision to build a major parish church for the new town on a very grand scale is amongst other things a reflection of the considerable disposable income available to the by-then well-established Norman ascendancy in Sussex.

What we see today at New Shoreham is grand enough and still dominates the little low-lying port, but it is only the east end of what was once a much larger Norman cruciform church, which originally had a long seven-bay nave, some fragmentary stumps and bumps of which are visible on the west side of the churchyard. The present church consists of one bay of the former nave, the original early 12th-century crossing tower and transepts, and the magnificent new five-bay aisled choir added over the course of several decades from around 1170 onwards. The west end was added in the early 18th century, re-using the badly weathered Norman west door. Quite when or why the nave fell down is unclear, and various explanations have been offered, including the results of French raids in 1628, Civil War damage from later in the 17th century, and a devastating storm in 1703 which caused severe destruction elsewhere in the town. Indeed it may well be the case that all these were component factors in a slow process of escalating decay.

The piers on the surviving older parts at the west end have typical early Norman scalloped capitals, quite distinct from the later decorative carving throughout the choir which was evidently built in different stages, the aisles first. They are walled with big round-arched blank arcading decorated in a most imaginative way with motifs enlarged from the vocabulary of late Romanesque architecture, including big triangular shapes like enlarged chevron details. At the west end of the south side these change into wonderfully fanciful abstract curvilinear forms, like those on the westerly arches of the choir arcades. There are nicely carved volutes on the capitals of the arcading, some of which have waterleaf decoration, and stone benches all the way along both sides. Look out for the three green-men on the bosses of the south aisle vault.

It was probably the success of the aisle-vaulting which led to the decision to construct a big stone vault above the choir, which in turn required the construction of the two pairs of supportive flying buttresses which were added outside above the aisles on either side at some time around 1180. At the same time the upper tower was remodelled and given pointed arches on the two upper stages, to great effect.

Looking east it is immediately apparent that the two sides of the choir are very different, creating a strangely hallucinatory effect. The main north arcade has alternating circular and octagonal piers with beautifully carved stiff-leaf in two tiers on the capitals, while the south arcade has compound piers. Above all this, the clerestory has much beautiful carved decorative detail. The main vault rests on several different kinds of brackets at the west end, but with luxuriantly rich stiff-leaf above the last two bays at the east end, as in the sacristy in Chichester cathedral and in the chapel of the Bishop's Palace. Everything is held together by the vaulting above, and by the design of the east wall, with its three big pointed lancet windows above three smaller arched windows, a nobly simple and effective composition. Very little restoration work took place before 1876, when new Norman-style windows replaced the later medieval aisle windows. The stained glass throughout is unmemorable.

Under the tower stands a magnificent square late-Norman font of Sussex marble set on a drum-shaped stem with four plain replacement corner-colonettes. Each side has different abstract decoration, including a strip of incised chevron, two big semi-circles side-by-side, a row of blank arches separated by twisted colonetttes, and four linked circles.

The north transept was dedicated to St George as a war memorial chapel in 1947, and has good plain semi-circular altar rails from around 1700 which were given at the time of the dedication.[1] It also houses a sequence of small Victorian and early 20th-century tablets commemorating members of the Hooper family, which are the only monuments inside the church apart from a few worn ledger-stones and the tops of a couple of Regency tablets visible behind cupboards in the south transept, and two rather indifferent 15th-century brasses of a man and a woman displayed on the wall of the south aisle.

The best monument at New Shoreham is an early 18th-century rococo marble cartouche, long exiled on the outside on the west end of the south aisle. This has a ferocious bat-winged skull as a corbel, but is now hopelessly badly weathered. It is exactly the kind of thing Victorian purists most disliked, but it must have looked wonderful in its original condition against the austere ashlar inside.

In the chapel at the east end of the south aisle there are nicely carved early 17th-century wooden altar rails with two doors which no longer meet. The rails are decorated with typical Jacobean balusters, lozenges, and so on. They have evidently been cut down from a larger ensemble. There is also a terrific small wooden credence-table on barley-sugar legs, with lots of carved decoration on the sides and front including a tiny Crucifixion flanked by the date 1638 and the letters 'TR'. Is it English? It certainly seems to be, though the twisted legs braced by flat, shaped stretchers underneath are of the late 17th century, perhaps

1. The Revd. F. Simpson, The Churches of Shoreham, Sussex, 1946, p.42.

replacing an unfashionably plain or damaged earlier support? It reflects the revival of interest in traditional liturgical furnishings at the time of Archbishop Laud. The extreme simplicity of the image of Christ on the Cross movingly suggests how little experience or opportunity English carvers had for undertaking such work in the wake of the Reformation, when all images of the story of Christ or the lives of the saints were widely considered to be superstitious. The churchyard has a few nice gravestones to sailors as one might well expect, but nothing special.

Getting there   National grid ref. TQ216051

◉ St Mary de Haura is on Church Street, about ten minutes walk from Shoreham-by-Sea station on the Brighton to Portsmouth line.

◉ Open daily 09.00 -17.00. Details on the website: **www.stmarydehaura.org.uk**

NORTH STOKE CHURCH

NORTH STOKE

Reached at the end of a long winding country lane from Houghton and set in a loop of the Arun, the village of North Stoke has all but vanished and the superb cruciform church which formerly served it is now in the care of the Churches Conservation Trust. Like the church at Coombes, its dedication is not recorded. Delightfully un-restored, with light flooding in from the clear glass windows, it is movingly eloquent of centuries of remote Sussex agricultural life. The wide nave is Norman, and the chancel was rebuilt in the early 13th-century with deeply recessed plain Early English lancet windows on both sides and a modern three-light window at the east end. This replaces an earlier window which had lost all its tracery by the 18th century. It now contains two fragments of 14th-century glass, a king and the Virgin Mary, which seem to derive from two separate larger compositions, and the window is flanked by two beautifully carved mid-13th-century stone brackets with lively swirling foliage. These once supported statues, and have tiny inquisitive faces on their undersides. On the north side of the chancel is a trefoil-headed piscina and three similarly arched recessed seats, or sedilia, the design of which reflects the rise of the underlying land.

The transepts are late 13th century, with much instructive contemporary window tracery. On the west wall of the south transept is a long stone seat below two tall blank arches which meet quite high up in a carved animal-head corbel which seems to represent a sheep or perhaps a ram. It is probably re-used from elsewhere in the former Norman church. There is also a well-preserved piscina in the south wall of the south transept, where the priest washed his hands when saying mass at a former altar. This retains its original internal credence-shelf.

The chancel arch was widened a little later and rests on octagonal responds with big niches on both sides facing west, in front of which there would once have been separate altars. On the north side there is a small human hand carved as if reaching from behind to hold up that side of the arch. It is doubtless the hand of the mason who carved these stones, a nice human touch which it is instructive to compare to the earlier Romanesque painted figure under the chancel arch at Coombes (*see p. 35*), straining to bear his similar load.

Above the chancel arch are ghostly shadows of 14th-century decorative painting with swirling patterns of flowers and foliage of a kind which evidently inspired the Sussex artist Lambert Barnard when he came to decorate the vaults at Boxgrove (*see p. 24*) and in the Lady Chapel of Chichester Cathedral in the early 16th century. A few smudges of colour also remain inside the recesses flanking the chancel arch, but enough to make it clear that this kind of work was never brightly coloured or obtrusive. The idea that the walls of medieval churches were once ablaze with garish colour is one of the many fantasies entertained by the Victorians, and bears no relation to the widespread evidence which shows that most medieval wall-painting consisted of earth colours and subtly modulated half-tones, in keeping with everything else we know about medieval art.

High above, the original plain timber roofing of the nave and south transept is exposed to great effect. As Ian Nairn commented, in some ways 'this little church can teach more about the medieval spirit of working than a cathedral.'[1] There is no crossing-tower, and the church's only bell is housed in a shingled timber bell-cote perched endearingly on the east side of the north transept roof.

A stylish black and white marble Regency-Gothic tablet on the south side of the chancel commemorates John and Elizabeth Sayres who died

---

1. *Ian Nairn and Niklaus Pevsner, The Buildings of England, Sussex 1965, p. 284.*

respectively in 1820 and 1809, and their only child John, who died aged 27 in 1818 when his widowed father was 70. Apart from a few worn ledger-stones there are no other surviving monuments at North Stoke, and in a way the whole church might be considered as a memorial to the countless generations of the 'faithful departed' who worshipped here. At the west end however there is a magnificent bulbous lead-lined font of Pulborough sandstone from about 1200, in which centuries of local parishioners were baptised. Like the fonts at East Marden and Stedham it quietly echoes the form of a humble communion chalice. Its position in relation to the plain late-13th-century triple-lancet window in the west wall behind is especially memorable.

Getting there   National grid ref. TQ019108

◗ North Stoke is 5 miles (8 kilometres) north of Arundel off the B2139 at Houghton and 3 miles (5 kilometres) from Amberley station on the London to Chichester line.

◗ Open daily. In the care of The Churches Conservation Trust.

◗ Details on the website: **www.visitchurches.org.uk**

ST PETER

RACTON

S et in rolling countryside on the Hampshire border some few kilometres north-west of Chichester, St Peter's church at Racton is a thoroughly delightful small country church with a 12th-century nave and a 13th-century chancel without aisles or chancel arch. A small shingled bell-cote is perched on top of the west end. The open timber roof looks just like the inside of an inverted ship, with an elaborately traceried tympanum supporting the large, lively Royal Arms of George II which are painted with rustic vigour, bursting with Hanoverian self-confidence. There are many things to see including a good though re-tooled plain late Norman tub font with neat roll-moulding around the rim, raised on two modern octagonal steps, as well as some interesting medieval carving.

There is an exceptionally fine five-light east window of 1918 by Christopher Whall (*1849-1924*) commemorating two local brothers who were both killed in action in 1916 aged 19 and 20. On the outside of the window are two carved escutcheons of the Gunter and Bohun families. Whall taught at the Central School in London and at the Royal College of Art, and was much the most gifted English stained-glass designer working in the Arts and Crafts tradition. He was responsible for other beautiful Sussex windows at Steyning and Milland, and an excellent window by his daughter Veronica can also be seen at Amberley (*see p.17*). There are several good carved 18th-century gravestones in the churchyard, including one to Mrs Liza Cooke (*died 1777*), with a tiny coffin flanked by curtains pulled back by two small energetic angels, one of whom sounds the trumpet of the General Resurrection. But it is the three fine monuments ranged along the north wall of the chancel that one visits Racton to see, and they make an unusually beautiful and instructive sequence despite the regrettable recent repainting of the early-17th-century tablet at the east end.

Dating from the mid-16th century, the handsome canopied wall monument on the left commemorates members of the local Gunter family, which had held the manor since the early 14th century. It is very much like a substantial piece of late medieval domestic furniture translated into limestone, and is of the same general family as nearby tombs at Boxgrove (*see p. 24*), West Wittering (*see p. 73*) and elsewhere, although the decorative detail here is a little less sophisticated. They were doubtless all made locally, perhaps in a workshop in Chichester.

The Gunter monument has a tomb-chest with three shields in decorated panels separated by two upright niches which doubtless once housed statues of saints. On the back wall is a touchingly rural relief of a husband and wife together with their children in two groups, on either side of a central standing figure of the Risen Christ. This can only have survived the ravages of the Reformation by being protected, perhaps under a layer of plaster, reflecting enduring traditions of local piety in the face of Puritan opposition. The canopy is set on a flat arch with prettily carved tendrils entwining the initials 'I' and 'G' on the front spandrels, together with a frieze of vine-trail ornament and some nice Renaissance decoration, including *putti* and griffins flanking shields on the front. The top is crested with fleur-de-lys and anthemion, and rounded off on the front with three big confident decorated finials. The east end is blank, suggesting that it once stood against a wall, probably doubling as an Easter Sepulchre at the east end of the sanctuary.

On the far right is a hanging freestone wall-monument commemorating Sir George Gunter, who died in 1624, and his wife Ursula. This has two kneeling figures facing one another on either side of a prayer-desk in an arched recess. It is local work, following fashions set in

London, but with its own distinct Sussex accent. A plain cornice on top supports a central upright achievement of arms above a timeless winged cherub-head, flanked by two charmingly rustic standing allegorical figures of Justice and Mercy, looking very much like local girls dressed up to perform in a contemporary masque or pageant. Until recently it retained its original colouring but alas no more after heavy and unsubtle repainting in the 1990s. Sir George was the grandfather of the celebrated Colonel George Gunter who with his cousin Thomas played such an instrumental role in the escape of the young Charles II by sea to France from Shoreham after the Battle of Worcester in 1651. A local legend that Charles stayed overnight at the farmhouse adjacent to the church is unfounded, although it seems his companion, the glamorous, fool-hardy libertine Viscount Wilmot, did indeed stay there in the final stages of the royal escape.[1]

Between these two tombs is the small but absolutely first-rate London-made marble standing wall monument to Sir Charles Gunter Nicoll who died aged 29 in 1733. This includes a superb white marble bust as good as any of its date in England and it could well be by Rysbrack, though like so many unsigned monuments its authorship is uncertain. Set up by his widow Elizabeth, it consists of a cool grey altar with a framed inscription plate on the front, on which rests a small black sarcophagus on white plinths. This carries the bust against a beautifully framed arched black marble background with scrolly side volutes, and an arched pediment on top. This in turn supports a finely carved heraldic cartouche flanked by two small plain round-lidded urns. Sir Charles's helm and gauntlets are suspended above. The epitaph describes him as:

> *a compleat and accomplish'd Gentleman, / Amiable in his Person, / Gracefull in his Address. / In Private, / He was easy, affable, condesending; / In Publick, / He was steady, uniform, consistent; / Favour'd by his Prince, / And a Friend to his Country.*

In an important decision on the part of the Chichester Consistory Court in October 2001, a faculty was refused to one of Nicoll's descendents who

---

1. *Richard Ollard, The Escape of Charles II after the Battle of Worcester, 1966.*

had wanted to remove the bust to his London home. This explicitly rejected an unfortunate 1999 precedent concerning the fate of a bust in the church of St Mary and St Nicholas at Wilton in Wiltshire (*5 Ecc. LJ 211*). The Chancellor found that the bust 'was an integral part of "a scheme of decoration" within the church and as such was a fixture rather than a mere chattel', and thus not disposable. The monument must have sighed with relief, as did everyone concerned with the protection of church monuments in England.

Finally you should look out for the nice small upright black and white Grecian tablet on the south wall of the chancel, which commemorates Mr and Mrs William Hipkin (*died 1828 and 1849*) with a small draped urn looking back to the fashions of their youth in the Regency period rather than to contemporary Victorian taste.

Getting there   National grid ref. SU779092

◉ Racton is on the B2147 about 7 miles (11 kilometres) north-west of Chichester.

◉ Open daylight hours. Details on the website: **www.octagon-parishes.org.uk**

ST MARY THE VIRGIN

RINGMER

Surrounded by a well-tended churchyard, St Mary at Ringmer in East Sussex is a substantial and well-maintained medieval village church which, like so many others, has been frequently enlarged and patched up over the centuries. The Springett family added a chapel to the south side of the chancel in around 1500, and a Lady Chapel was added on the north side in the 1530s with a later Jacobean ceiling with nice blue and white vine-trails on the beams. The plain two-stage west tower (*1884-85*) was built by Ewan Christian, and the church is entered through a picturesque late medieval south porch. Inside there are many good fittings and furnishings including hatchments on either side of the chancel arch, charity boards recording ancient bequests to local causes, and the lively Royal Arms of George III painted on board in the south chancel chapel. You should also look out for several good plain black marble ledger-stones on the floor.

Hanging in the south chapel is an excellent small upright alabaster wall-monument to Harbert Springett who died in 1620, described on his epitaph as: 'A friend to vertue, a lover of learning / of prudence great, of Justice a furtherer'. He is represented kneeling at a draped prayer-desk under a shallow panelled arch decorated with rosettes and flanked by two free-standing obelisks with finials. Above is a small open pediment flanking an upright achievement of arms with a small central pediment on top, from which, most unusually at this date, gilded flames emerge. Unfortunately his effigy has been over-enthusiastically repainted in modern times, creating a harsh effect which has long been popular with restorers but which sadly bears little relation to the original subtle use of paint on monuments in the early 17th century.

In the north chapel is a small damaged hanging alabaster wall-monument to Elizabeth Jefferay who also died in 1620, aged 39. This has two well carved but now hand-less kneeling figures facing one another across the plinth of a former prayer desk, flanked by plain panelled pilasters. Immediately underneath this is an inscription plate to Richard Mascall and his ten-year-old daughter Jane, both of whom died in 1631. This is all that now survives from a former monument set up by his wife Frances, and contains an unusually eloquent and touching epitaph describing how she made the memorial: 'Too Little To Express His Desert Or Her Affection'.

On the west wall of the south chapel is an important small upright black and white marble hanging wall-monument to Colonel William Springett who died in l643. A fanatical Puritan and iconoclast, he was a deputy-lieutenant of Sussex. According to a memoir written by his equally Puritan wife, he had:

> a great zeal against superstition, encouraging his soldiers and requiring them
> to break down idolatrous pictures and crosses, and going into steeple houses
> [e.g. churches] [he] would take the surplices and distribute them to big bellied
> women. When he was upon the service of searching popish houses, whatever
> crucifixes, beads, and such like trumpery, he found, if they were never so rich,
> he destroyed them, and reserved not one of them for its comeliness or costly
> workmanship, nor saved anything for his own use.[1]

He even took his sword to a painting of the Crucifixion inside a Protestant colleague's private house. He died aged only 23 from an unspecified illness during the siege of Arundel Castle, and his monument at Ringmer is one of a small number of surviving shrines to Puritan martyrs of the Civil War period. Perhaps by Edward Marshall, and certainly a good

---

1. *Julie Spraggon, Puritan Iconoclam during the English Civil War, 2003.*

London-made piece of work, it includes a rather feminine long-haired bust, his eyes cast upwards, in a black oval recess in a white moulded frame between flat black pilasters. The arched pediment above has a carved helm on top with gauntlets draped on either side.

On the north wall of the sanctuary is a magnificent white marble Baroque cartouche commemorating Richard Wynne (*died 1679*). It includes a good small garlanded blazing urn on top, and an excellent sad cherub-head with rising wings. The whole thing has an almost Art Nouveau style about it which one associates with the mason-sculptor Jasper Latham (*c.1640-93*). At the east end of the north wall of the south chapel is another superbly carved white marble Stuart Baroque tablet, set up by Dame Lucy Whalley in memory of her husband Sir Herbert, who died in 1689, aged 28. With a central inscription on suspended drapery, it rests on a beautiful cherub-head corbel, and has two kneeling mourning cherubs on top and excellent falls of flowers on both sides, alas badly damaged on the right. The level of carving is every bit as good as anything from the Restoration period, which is saying a lot.

There are many other smaller things to look out for at Ringmer, including a nice Adam-ish tablet to Richard Shadwell who died in 1785, which has an attractive two-handled Grecian urn on top. Last, but by no means least, is the larger marble wall monument in the south aisle to Ensign H. D. Crunden who died in action in 1793. Probably by Sir Richard Westmacott, it has a very good standing figure of Fortitude above a military still-life, and a telling inscription:

> *Peace to the ashes of the Young and Brave / Who sunk thro Duty, to an early Grave / Who to his Country, gave Health's little store, / Nor Ceas'd the Boon till Life's short Scene was o're / Ye softer Souls; whom human lives refine, / Oft as ye bend at Pity's sacred Shrine, / Here breathe the Sigh, with Tears bedew this Stone, / And with a Father's Feelings blend your own.*

Getting there   National grid ref. TQ445125

❯ Ringmer is 2 miles (3 kilometres) north of Lewes on the B2192.

❯ Regular buses from Lewes.

❯ The church is open daily from 10.00-14.00 and 14.30-16.30.

❯ Details on the website **www.ringmerchurch.org.uk**

ST MARY

✝ SOMPTING

S ussex is particularly rich in Saxon churches largely because there was so little population growth in the Middle Ages outside the few thriving coastal ports, and hence little pressure or resources for substantial rebuilding. For most of its history, Sompting was an isolated farming settlement on a former Roman road running along the foot of the South Downs, and it was this remoteness which contributed most to the preservation of the building we see today. A total of around 60 inhabitants in 1086 rose to only 450 by 1800. In the 19th century the parish was known for its orchards where figs were grown behind the shelter of tall flint walls, many of which survive. In his old age Byron and Shelley's friend Edward John Trelawny lived here and grew figs, claiming they were the equal to those of Italy.

St Mary is a substantial Saxon church celebrated for the starkly gabled top to its tower known as a 'Rhenish helm' because of its resemblance to towers at Andernach, Coblentz and Cologne, but unique in England. It was erected in three stages in the course of the 11th century, with vertical pilasters on the corners and the middle of each side, with a horizontal string-course a third of the way up. The internal timbers are 14th century but they seem to follow an earlier design reflected in surviving Saxon joist-holes in the walls. Two of the windows are decorated inside with carved heads. Though reduced by some 27 feet in 1762, the tower still raises its head proudly above trees.

The church is entered through a 12th-century doorway inside a small 16th-century porch leading directly into the south transept which was originally built as an autonomous chapel at a lower level to the rest of the building. It takes a moment or two to register the fact that one is facing the south side of the nave which is reached by a flight of four steps. To the west, the rounded Saxon tower arch rests on massive imposts decorated with coiled forms rather like unfolding bracken and enclosing what look rather like pomegranates. These are flanked by worn capitals on either side with tiers of tiny leaves. The nave and chancel were rebuilt after the church was granted to the Knights Templar in 1154, and they follow the former Saxon ground-plan but without a separating chancel arch. The nave has a blocked north doorway with worn Romanesque carved animal head-stops on either side, and a grimacing animal-head at the apex.

The Templars also added two transepts. The north transept contains two chapels of its own to the east with a vault above them resting on a splendid head-stop corbel on the east wall. Of uncertain date, it closely resembles the head-stop of the second bay on the south nave-arcade at Steyning. The vault has two nicely carved bosses with stiff-leaf foliage. On the other side of the nave, the lower south transept of c.1180 has its own tiny eastern chancel which now serves as a baptistery and is reached through a round arch resting on capitals carved with delightful simplified acanthus-leaf decoration. Its vault rests on small waterleaf capitals.

On the seizure of the Templars' estates in 1308, the church passed into the hands of the Knights Hospitaller, who added a chapel on the north side of the tower. This survived for only a century or so, and the ruins were re-used in the 20th century to form the basis of a new vestry. The entire church was restored in 1853, when most of the original stone surfaces were scraped, creating a rather misleadingly uniform effect.

Various pieces of attractively carved Saxon stonework were re-used by the Normans. These include the narrow borders to the aumbry at the east end of the chancel which is decorated with a woven basket-work motif terminating in leafy trefoils. On the south wall is a piscina with a triangular head decorated with similar basket-work and more lily-like trefoils. Set into the east wall of the south transept is a small well-preserved early 12th-century carved stone panel of a standing saint with a book on a lectern and a crozier to his left. The forms are distinctively rounded and archaic.

On the north wall of the nave another carved stone slab is displayed on a bracket at right-angles to the wall in order to show both its sides. On the west-facing side is a fragment of 11th-century arcading with big circular plant forms, perhaps from the original chancel screen. This was turned round and re-used in the early 13th century, when an excellent figure of Christ in Majesty was carved on the other side. He is shown seated in a mandorla with his right hand raised in blessing and symbols of the four Evangelists at the corners. Sadly, the entire relief has been badly vandalised.

In the chapel at the east end of the south chancel is a plain circular Sussex-marble Norman tub-font with a hollow chamfer around the bottom edge. It rests on a modern plinth and was evidently enthusiastically re-polished in the 19th century. This may seem like vandalism today but it does at least serve to show what such fonts looked like when new. There is also another small badly weathered font with figurative scenes at the east end of the nave.

Apart from a few minor 18th-century marble tablets on the north wall of the north transept the only monument of note is a locally made freestone canopied wall-tomb on the north side of the chancel. This commemorates Richard Burre, a London merchant who held the lease of the old rectory and died in 1527. It now consists of a recessed tomb-chest decorated with shields and niches, and was intended to be used as an Easter Sepulchre. On the back wall there was probably once a carved religious scene of the type which survives on contemporary monuments at West Wittering (*see p. 73*) and elsewhere in West Sussex, but of this nothing now remains.

Getting there   National grid ref. TQ 161 056

◉ St Mary is just north of the A27 at Sompting between Worthing and Lancing.

◉ 3 miles (5 kilometres) from Lancing station on the Brighton to Portsmouth line.

◉ Open daily. Details on Diocesan website: **www.diochi.org.uk**

ST PETER & ST PAUL

WEST WITTERING

As remote as anywhere in southern England two centuries ago, the villages on the western end of the Selsey peninsular are now cheerful holiday spots reached via tree-lined lanes that straggle through lush farm-land perched just above sea-level. The comparatively large size of the parish church at West Wittering is associated with the proximity of Cakeham Manor House which was begun in the 12th century as a country seat for the Bishops of Chichester and retains a fine Tudor brick tower which gazes placidly down across the greedily land-hungry coast-line. The churchyard is surrounded by typical protective Sussex flint walls, and there are several forcefully stylised richly lichen-clad 18th-century gravestones, including one from the 1730s to members of the Purdie family, with a terrific skull in profile on top, and another commemorating Thomas Napper (*died 1757*) with a moon-faced cherub head peering out above a solitary bone.

Turning to the interior, patches of herringbone masonry high up in the north wall of the nave reveal the church's Saxon origins, before the Normans added a four-bay south aisle in around 1200 with alternating round and octagonal piers. The tower is unusual in being located on the north side, and was built in the 13th century, as were the south chapel and chancel. The date is apparent from the plain twin-lancet design of the much-restored east windows, and from the trefoil-headed piscina in the south wall. There is a substantial empty recess in the east wall of the south chapel, which has been interpreted as the base of an older window but which may have housed a former shrine to St Richard of Chichester which the church is known to have contained. He stayed frequently at Cakeham, where he was held responsible for two miracles, though his principal shrine was in Chichester cathedral. A battered but finely carved Purbeck marble coffin lid with a raised Cross and an incised bishop's crozier was perhaps the top of the saint's former reliquary. This was discovered in 1875 under the floor of the sanctuary in front of the altar, where it was doubtless hidden for protection during the Reformation.

At the west end of the south arcade of the nave is an early Norman tub-shaped font, of a type found widely in Sussex at Bignor, Selling, Woolbeding and elsewhere. It consists of a large, plain, deep limestone lead-lined drum, set on a wide modern circular plinth, but is unfortunately rather hemmed in by Victorian seating and hence difficult to fully appreciate. A rather ugly conical Victorian wooden cover doesn't improve things. Happily, the much restored choir stalls in the chancel retain one original medieval misericord decorated with a bishop's head and roses. There are also a few heavily restored old benches with fleurs-de-lys finials, and good Jacobean communion rails in front of the altar with a frieze of nicely turned balusters. In the south chapel is a plain early 17th-century wooden communion table, hidden behind a large framed panel of rather unsympathetic late 20th-century embroidery.

On the north side of the chancel are two important freestone monuments to William Ernley (*died 1545*) and his first wife Elizabeth (*died 1528*). They now stand side by side under low, flat, recessed arches but old prints show the later tomb originally stood against the east wall at right-angles to the earlier one. Hers to the west is the earlier of the pair and is still purely Gothic in design, with a badly defaced but lively central relief of Christ rising from his tomb, flanked by heraldic escutcheons. The tomb-chest below has tracery and saints in niches on the front including St George slaying the dragon, and St Roche. It probably originally also served as an Easter Sepulchre.

William's tomb to the east was set up by his second wife Bridget, and has a lively carved relief with kneeling figures on either side of the standing figure of the resurrected Christ displaying his five wounds. On the front of the tomb-chest below is a beautiful carving of the Annunciation, showing the head of God the Father appearing from clouds and releasing the Holy Spirit as a dove above the kneeling angel Gabriel on the left, with the Virgin Mary kneeling at a prayer-desk on the right. Between them stands a bulgy two-handled vase of lilies with a tiny image of Christ crucified against the flowers. This is one of only 15 known versions of this image in late medieval art, all of which are of British origin.[1] It seems to have been connected to the annual celebration of the Feast of the Annunciation on March 25. Known as Lady Day, it was widely believed in Britain to have been the date of the Crucifixion.

Both sides of the canopy are decorated with delightful early Renaissance arabesques including podgy little cherubs, vases, and so on, very much like the busy decoration on so much contemporary secular furniture. Such Italianate imagery was carved by men who had never seen Italian Renaissance sculpture with their own eyes, but were familiar with some aspects of its decorative language indirectly from contemporary French and Flemish prints, which they translated with a charmingly strong Sussex accent. Its former cornice with carved cherubs and mermaids was alas destroyed in the 19th century.

The Ernleys were a Catholic family and their tombs belong to a cluster of related contemporary monuments in West Sussex. Such religious imagery was extremely vulnerable to Puritan iconoclasts, and this rare group must have been protected by local parishioners, doubtless at some risk to themselves. They were all locally made, perhaps in Chichester, and the delightful rustic traditions of West Sussex carving evidently endured well into Georgian times, as one can see from the gravestones outside.

---

1. *Simon Watney, The Lily-Crucifixion in late Medieval English Art, Pagans and Christians-Antiquity to the Middle Ages, ed. Lauren Gilmour, 2007.*

Getting there   National grid ref. SZ777984

⦿ West Wittering is 4 miles (6 kilometres) from Nutbourne station on the Brighton to Portsmouth line.

⦿ Bus services run from Chichester, about 11.2 kilometres south.

⦿ Information about visiting from The Revd. J. B. Williams tel. 01243 514057.

⦿ Details on Diocesan website: **www.diochi.org.uk**

ST MARY THE VIRGIN

WILLINGDON

Like most of the villages on the immediate north side of the Downs between Brighton and Eastbourne, Willingdon consists of a long straggling High Street leading to the foot of the sharply rising escarpment. The layout of the parish church of St Mary the Virgin is rather unusual, but it is not difficult to work out how it arrived at its current shape. Unlike the towers of most churches which are either at the west end or between the nave and chancel, Willingdon's sturdy 13th-century example with its rather squat broach-spire stands almost completely detached at the north-west corner of the present church, its buttresses patched up with brick over the years.

It originally opened into the west end of the nave of the former Norman church, on the site of which the present north aisle was built in the early 14th century, at the same time as the addition of a much larger new nave to the south. In effect, the church moved southwards, leaving the tower where it was. A new chancel was added some 60 or so years later. Just to confuse matters, the south doorway into the south porch dates from around 1300, and must have been salvaged and re-used when the older building was demolished.

The church was hit by two bombs in 1944 but was sympathetically restored and reordered inside, and the damage was ultimately much less severe than that caused by overzealous Victorian restorers in so many other Sussex churches.

The interior is light and spacious with fine open kingpost roofs throughout, as at nearby Folkington and elsewhere. The Ratton family chapel at the east end of the north aisle is divided off by good 19th-century traceried wooden parclose screens, with a fine wrought-iron gate,designed by the Reverend Harry Copsey around 1943, which gives access to the chancel. The noble carved wooden rood under the chancel arch was designed by Sir Ninian Comper, and given by him to the church in 1954. There is also a good west gallery of 1953 with the Royal Arms of Elizabeth II on the front. Beneath this stands an excellent square 14th-century font of local greenstone on a square traceried stem.

In the east window of the north chapel are six attractive golden-yellow panels of heraldic glass dated 1622 with the arms of the Parker family commemorating marriages from 1588 onwards, but most of the other glass in the church was blown out in World War II. Happily the later glass is uniformly good, including an excellent St Michael in the north aisle, and a 1947 war memorial window in the south aisle, both designed by Hugh Easton and made by Hendra of Harpenden. The latter includes three servicemen kneeling in prayer against the background of the South Downs, a motif borrowed from Duncan Grant's 1943 mural decoration on the chancel arch at nearby Berwick church. Look out for the fine 1948 memorial window to Eustace Tanner in the north aisle, with St George and St Christopher, designed by Hugh Easton. The east window is a characteristically beautiful work by the much-neglected Christopher Webb, with Christ in glory flanked by St Wilfrid and St Richard of Chichester. Webb's windows may also be seen at St Saviour, Eastbourne (*see p.42*) and at St Andrew, Hove (*see p.52*).

Most of the surviving monuments are in the north chapel and they make a very fine group, beginning with the small alabaster tablet on the east wall to Mrs Elinar Parker (*died 1598*), who lived to the great age of 83. On the north wall of the sanctuary is another good alabaster hanging monument to her younger son Sir John Parker (*died 1617*), which includes a particularly well-carved image of him kneeling in armour. Look out for the excellent green-man on the lower part of the frame, an unusual motif in the 17th century. Back in the north chapel is the fine London-made monument to his older brother Sir Nicholas Parker (*died 1619*) together with his three wives Jane, Elizabeth and Katherine. He was a soldier who served in the Low Countries, and was later Governor of Plymouth from 1601 to 1603. He is represented by a recumbent effigy on a tomb-chest with his three wives (in freestone) seen kneeling in relief on the front facing east.

At the east end of the north wall of the sanctuary is an attractive small classical black and white marble tablet to the splendidly named Lady Margaret Wildegoose (*died 1656*), which was set up by her nephew George Parker. Half-way down the north aisle is the superb standing marble monument to Sir Thomas Parker (*died 1663*) and other members of his family. This is very similar to surviving contemporary monuments in Westminster Abbey and at Tonbridge and Hunton in Kent, with a large gadrooned urn on a tall narrow altar, raised on a black plinth, flanked by two small heraldic cartouches on the wall behind. Writing in *The Buildings of England* (*1965, p.629*) Ian Nairn concluded quite wrongly that it is of the 18th century. A later inscription on one side recording dates of death until 1708 may have misled him.

Back in the north chapel there is an excellent oval cartouche to Dame Katharine Nutt (*died 1700*), and a big standing reredos monument to Sir George and Lady Mary Parker (*died 1726 and 1727*). One would like to know more of her life, given her description as:

> a Lady, of an Exceeding good Character, / Prudent, Pious, and Charitable.
> / In the midst of Family Misfortunes / Showed a great Example, of Meekness
> and Humility, / of Patience and Resignation, to the Will of God.

The family title died with her husband.

On the east wall is a fabulously beautiful Baroque cartouche commemorating William Parker (*died 1727*). This has a Latin epitaph on fringed drapery, suspended from two central well-carved winged cherub-heads, with a bravura escutcheon on top with mantling, trumpets and falls of flowers. There are two more superb winged cherub heads on either side at the base, flanking a delightful floral still-life.

The sequence continues with good later monuments to Nathaniel and Philadelphia Trayton (*died 1757 and 1755*) and a typically restrained Regency tablet commemorating Mrs Charlotte Thomas who died in Lisbon in 1800 at the age of 20, the stylish simplicity of which is in marked contrast to the ornate Victorian Gothic tablet to Inigo Thomas (*died 1867*). Finally the small brown alabaster tablet to Captain Alan Thomas (*died 1891*) with traditional 17th-century style decoration is a good example of the brief revival of interest in Jacobean taste and style at the turn of the 20th century.

Getting there   National grid ref. TQ589024

⊙ Willingdon is south of the A2270, 2 miles (3 kilometres) west of Eastbourne.

⊙ Buses from Eastbourne station.

⊙ Parish office tel. 01323 501763.

⊙ Open daily. Details on Diocesan website: **www.diochi.org.uk**

ST THOMAS THE MARTYR

WINCHELSEA

An ancient foundation, sufficiently important to have been a royal dockyard in the reign of King John, the port of Old Winchelsea suffered from disastrous storm-damage and coastal erosion from the 1230s onwards, and was all but washed away in 1287. As a result of this prolonged period of severe climate-change the Rother shifted its course away from the former river-mouth port of Romney to its present route out to sea past Rye. Under the royal patronage of Edward I a new town was planned on a headland several miles inland on the opposite side of the wide and newly inundated bay. Originally surrounded by water on three sides, New Winchelsea was intended to serve the Bordeaux wine trade and was laid out on a grid-plan on the grandest scale. It subsequently proved a popular port of embarkation for pilgrims to the shrine of St James at Compostella in Spain.

From the start a mighty new church was intended for the apex of the hill, and as at Boxgrove (*see p. 24*) and New Shoreham (*see p. 56*) it is the eastern end of a formerly much larger building which survives today as the parish church of St Thomas the Martyr. The ruins of the original crossing-tower and transepts may still be seen immediately to the west, but it remains unclear whether or not the nave was ever completed. The town was subjected to severe French raids in 1340, 1359 and 1360. They returned to fire the place in 1377, and again in 1380, from which it never fully recovered. Attacks continued well into the 15th century, by which time the harbour had in any case become almost entirely silted up, and the port was finally closed. In 1575 there were only 60 surviving households in the town. According to Daniel Defoe, by the late 17th century it was recorded:

> rather the skeleton of an ancient city than a real town, where the antient gates stand near three miles from one another over the fields, and where the ruins are so well bury'd, that they have made good corn fields over the streets, and the plow goes over the foundations, nay, over the first floors of the houses, and where nothing of a town but the destruction of it seems to remain.[1]

Three of the ancient gates still stand, providing access to what is now little more than a village.

Yet what remains of the church of St Thomas is of cathedral-scale ambition and quality and seems to wear its only-too-visible wounds and scars with pride. Moreover in a county not rich in 14th-century architecture it provides much the best surviving example of the Decorated style. It was presumably begun around 1290, but what we see today is almost entirely of the early 14th century, and consists of a four-bay chancel with side-aisles originally ending on the south side in a Lady Chapel, and on the north side in a chapel dedicated like the churches at Brighton and Old Shoreham to St Nicholas of Myra. These dedications have subsequently been reversed. An adjacent free-standing tower of uncertain purpose was pulled down as late as 1790. The chancel was securely walled off in the 16th century much as we see it today, and the present west porch reconstructed from older materials. Save for the sanctuary, the interior was robbed of its original plasterwork by misguided 19th-century restorers, as at Withyham and elsewhere, and to equally unfortunate effect. Yet in spite of everything the interior is as magnificent as that of any parish church in Sussex.

This is largely a matter of scale and materials, each of the soaring piers being surrounded by four slim dark Sussex marble columns, which are also used to flank the vast windows, creating an effect of great

---

1. *op. cit., p. 130.*

transparency. The fittings are equally sumptuous, including the richly crocketed sedilia and piscina in the chancel, and the still more magnificent sedilia and piscina in the south chapel, with much ogee decoration and exquisitely carved head-stops. This splendour is more than matched by the two sequences of early 14th-century monuments lined up along both sides of the church, and as good as any of their date in England. Against the north wall are three fabulously canopied and decorated freestone tombs housing three recumbent effigies which have often wrongly been taken to be older than the present building and to have come from the former church at Old Winchelsea. Made of dark Purbeck marble, they are of superb quality and probably commemorate Robert Alard, his wife Isabel and his brother Henry.[2] Their restrained dignity is admirably amplified by the elaborately carved triangular gables under which they lie, decorated with huge rippling leaves, together with a wealth of lively head-stops and a magnificent green-man.

The two monuments on the north side are even more elaborate, and continuous at the eastern end with the adjacent piscina and sedilia, from which the tomb on the left of around 1312 is separated by a bracket supported by a crouching dwarf. In spite of the stylistic differences involved, this is closer in spirit to the lively 12th-century painting of a crouching man supporting the north side of the chancel arch at Coombes (*see p.35*) than to anything in the intervening century. The stone effigy with a lion at its feet is now thought to represent Stephen Alard. According to tradition the two head-stops flanking the gable represent Edward I (*died 1307*) on the left side, and his wife Queen Margaret on the right. The gable of the second monument immediately to the west rests on head-stops supposedly represents Edward II and Queen Isabella, the latter sadly worn. It houses a magnificent stone effigy in military costume, his feet resting by a lion, and his head raised on pillows supported by a small damaged seated angel. It is now thought to represent William Maufe who died between 1306 and 1311.[3] All the decorative detail is of the highest order.

---

2. Blair, Goodall & Lankester, *The Winchelsea Tombs Reconsidered, Church Monuments, Vol. XV,* 2000.
3. *ibid.*

One only wishes that the same could be said of the stained glass windows installed throughout the church between 1928 and 1933. They were commissioned by Sir Robert Younger, later Baron Blanesburgh (*1861-1946*), a successful Scottish barrister, Queen's Counsel and regrettably influential wealthy local resident. For these he turned to Douglas Strachen (*1875-1950*), an Aberdonian artist much given to crassly overblown symbolism. All the faces are distressingly badly drawn and everything is overlaid with a kind of clumsy instant Expressionism. Flagrantly disregarding the logic of the tracery which houses them and shockingly indifferent to their surroundings, including the monuments which shrink beneath them, the windows are frankly vulgar kitsch, and 40 years' acquaintance have not softened their unfortunate jarring impact for this viewer.

Strachan's harshly unattractive acidic colouring was seemingly influenced by his early mentor, enamellist James Cromer Watts, and his work entirely lacks the sensitivity to materials of contemporary Scottish designers such as Frances MacNair or Phoebe Traquair, let alone Charles Rennie Mackintosh and Margaret Mackintosh. Blanesburgh further blighted the church with the additional gift of a most inappropriately vast and hideous organ which was installed as a memorial to members of his family in 1931, entirely dominating the west wall. Looking at Christopher Webb's beautiful east windows at nearby Rye and his work at St Saviour, Eastbourne (*see p.42*), one may sense the enormity of the opportunity that was squandered here.

Getting there   National grid ref. TQ905173
❯ Winchelsea is about 2 miles (3 kilometres) from Rye train station on the Ashford to Brighton line, and is served by regular buses from Rye.
❯ Open daily. Details on Diocesan website: **www.diochi.org.uk**

ST MICHAEL & ALL ANGELS

WITHYHAM

Grandly positioned on a wooded hilltop near the Kent border, the parish church of St Michael and All Angels at Withyham was largely rebuilt after having been badly damaged by lightning in 1663. Withyham is the main mausoleum of the Sackville family whose principal country seat was at Knole near Sevenoaks in Kent. Sadly all the earlier monuments in the former family chapel to the north of the chancel were destroyed in the 1663 disaster. Its replacement has a splendid gold and azure ceiling and is separated from the chancel by magnificent 17th-century iron railings. The original 17th-century black and white marble flooring was misguidedly removed in the 19th century, together with the church's pews and pulpit, and south porch. Their replacements are sadly undistinguished. The apparently medieval octagonal stone font is actually 17th century, as proclaimed by the boldly carved date of 1666. Its traditional style suggests much about the mood of Restoration England and a determination to move on from the catastrophes of the Commonwealth and Interegnum.

Unfortunately the whole church was drastically over-restored in the 19th century and the interior feels correspondingly bleak. However it is not so much the architecture but the Sackville monuments that one comes to see. None of them are done any favours, however, by the now dungeon-like internal wall surfaces. Obtrusive dark grey cement pointing has been applied everywhere, producing a maddeningly ugly all-over crazy-paving effect, as in many other similarly over-zealously restored churches in the region. The effect of the re-pointing makes it very difficult to appreciate any of the interior architectural qualities of the church and also unfortunately distracts attention from the magnificent sequence of monuments. A moment's examination of the older mortar pointing outside reveals the enormity of the damage within.

Free-standing in the middle of the north chapel is the extraordinary 1677 monument to Thomas Sackville who died aged 13 in 1675, together with his parents, Richard Sackville, Fifth Earl of Dorset who died in l676, and his wife Frances, who completed the monument after her husband's death. By the Danish-born sculptor Caius Gabriel Cibber (*1630-1700*), its description as 'one of the noblest works of art in England' is not an over-statement.[1]

Set on a magnificent wide black marble plinth, it consists of a superb large black and white marble tomb-chest with charming reliefs of children on both sides, largely hidden by the life-size figures of their parents in front of them. The Earl and his Countess kneel, stricken, leaning on the chest for support. They make a touchingly young and handsome couple. By contrast the features of their eldest son Thomas are evidently idealised as he semi-reclines on top of the chest between them on a rolled up mat, resting his left hand on a magnificently carved skull on his lap. He seems to be struggling to sit upright, or perhaps he is collapsing back onto the mat? The pose is evidently experimental, and at the same time affecting. The overall effect of the ensemble is very Dutch, rather like a painting by Ter Boch re-imagined as sculpture. The original contract required that the design should be to the liking of the king's Principal Painter, the Dutch-trained Sir Peter Lely (*1618-80*), and one wonders if he might have had some say in its conception.

The fifth Earl died before the monument he had commissioned was installed. At the age of only 15 he had married Lady Frances Cranfield, daughter of the Earl of Middlesex, who is herself commemorated by a magnificent free-standing black and white marble monument by the

---

1. *Rupert Gunnis, Withyam Parish Church, n.d., p. 7.*

great mason-sculptor Nicholas Stone (*1586-1647*), which can be seen in St Benedict's Chapel, Westminster Abbey. Cibber had come to England during the Interregnum to work for Stone's son John, which may explain how he obtained the commission.

The Sackville monument is unique in Restoration England in its dramatic fusion of grandeur and intimacy, and constitutes a magnificent reworking of some of the most enduring traditions of late 16th- and earlier 17th-century funeral sculpture, including the rolled-up mat, the use of skulls, and the basic format of an effigy on a chest with kneeling figures in relief on its long sides. Moreover, the life-size kneeling figures update the anguished mourners seen beside the tomb-chests on earlier 17th-century monuments by Epiphanius Evesham at Lynsted and Otterden across the county border in Kent.

Its mood is immensely classical, yet with a hitherto unseen dramatic naturalism. Our attention is drawn to the family drama as a spectacle of intense pathos. In both its materials and style it sums up a strand of taste and feeling that goes back to the work of Nicholas Stone, whose monuments epitomised the sensibility of the court of Charles I, transferred across the Interregnum to the time of Charles II. Yet strangely neither Cibber nor anyone else pursued this new approach, and the monument thus appears to have been the end of one line rather than the beginning of another.

In almost any other church the later monuments would immediately be recognised for their consistently high quality, but here it must be said they rather struggle to compete with Cibber's quietly dominating masterpiece and the jarring effect of the surrounding walls. Taken together they are a remarkable expression of Regency taste. First comes a beautiful white marble 1802 tablet on the north wall to John Frederick, Third Duke of Dorset, with three big energetic *putti* busily draping garlands around an excellent portrait medallion on the front of an urn. It was made by Joseph Nollekens (*1737-1823*), whose popular and lucrative Neoclassical style was perfected when he worked as a restorer in Rome. Next comes an intensely poetic Grecian tablet to George John Frederick, Fourth Duke of Dorset (*died in 1815*) by John Flaxman (*1755-1826*), the Royal Academy's first Professor of Sculpture. It shows a robed woman seated by an urn on a plinth against which she rests her head on her right arm, with a portrait medallion above. The sequence ends with a monument to Arabella Diana, Fourth Duchess of Dorset (*died in 1825*), which was set up by her daughters, who are shown carved in Grecian costume kneeling by a draped urn. Here the sculptor, Sir Francis Chantrey (*1781-1841*), has raised the emotional temperature slightly. Finally you should not miss the simple slate epitaph by Reynolds Stone (*1909-79*) to the celebrated writer-gardener Vita Sackville-West, who died in 1962.

Getting there   National grid ref. TQ493355

◈ Withyham is midway between Tunbridge Wells and Uckfield on the B2110 by Hewkins Bridge, about 4 miles (6 kilometres) from Ashurst station on the Uckfield line.
◈ Information about visiting from the Revd. A.S. Leak, tel. 01892 770241.
◈ Details on the website: **www.withyham.org.uk**

Acknowledgements

I am grateful to all the incumbents, church-wardens and others who provided me with information about access and other matters relating to the churches discussed in these pages. I should also like to thank Neil Bartlett and Ivor Flint for driving me to otherwise inaccessible locations. I must thank my partner Glyn for his support and encouragement throughout this project.

Simon Watney, 2006

GLOSSARY

Aedicule A framed space between columns usually with a pediment above.

Altar A stone table used for the celebration of mass.

The Annunciation The appearance of the Angel Gabriel to the Virgin Mary informing her that she is to give birth to the son of God.

Arabesque A form of Renaissance surface decoration based on Roman prototypes, often with masks, candelabra, cherubs, and so on.

Arcade A row of free-standing arches supported on columns or piers.

Ashlar Smoothed-down masonry walling.

Aumbry A small cupboard, often recessed into a wall, usually on the north side of the chancel, used to house altar vessels used during mass.

Baldacchino A raised canopy usually with curtain pulled back at either side.

Baluster A short column or pillar, usually supporting railing, as on a staircase.

Baptistery A chapel or other space reserved for baptisms.

Baroque The dominant style of 17th-century art and design.

Battlement A parapet with regular indentations, typically found along the top of defensive castle walls or on the top of church towers.

Bell-cote A small free-standing roof structure housing a bell or bells.

Blind-arcading A row of arches supported on columns or piers against a wall.

Box-pews Pre-Victorian wooden church seating with tall surrounds to provide privacy and protect from draughts.

Bracket A support underneath and holding up a decorative object or architectural feature, often decorated.

Brass An incised memorial plate, often with an image of the deceased.

Broach-spire An octagonal spire rising from a square tower.

Capital The head of a column or pier, usually decorated.

Cartouche An ornately carved tablet usually with a central inscription.

Chamfer The blunting of any sharp edge between two surfaces, often in the form of a forty-five-degree angle, or a concave groove.

Chancel The east end of a church housing the altar.

Chancel arch The main arch separating the nave from the chancel inside a church.

Chantry A chapel commemorating an individual or family in which masses were said for their souls.

Chevron Zig-zag moulding, usually Norman.

Clerestory The upper storey of a nave with windows to admit light.

Colonettes Small columns.

Communion Table A moveable wooden table used in Protestant churches for the celebration of Holy Communion.

Corbel Another word for a bracket, supporting an object against a wall from below.

Corbel-Table A row of corbels, often decorated with animal and human heads, supporting the eaves of a roof. Usually along the outside of a nave or tower.

Cornice A moulded ledge along the top of a monument or other decorative feature. Also rather confusingly used to refer to a strip of moulding between the top of a wall and a ceiling.

Credence-Table A table to support ritual objects used at mass.

Crossing-tower A tower built between the nave and chancel of a church, often flanked by transepts.

Cruciform Cross-shaped.

Decorated style The major artistic and architectural style of the early 14th century.

Dog-tooth A widely-used late Norman and Early English decorative motif consisting of diagonal stars with a raised central point.

Early English The early Gothic style of the 13th century, using simple pointed arches.

Easter sepulchre A recess or container used to house an image of Christ during Easter celebrations.

Escutcheon A coat of heraldic arms.

Finial A decorative pinnacle on top of a gable or canopy.

Font An object housing water for the purpose of baptism.

Gadrooning A row of raised curves, often used on the edging of shelves.

Gallery A raised area with seating, usually supported on columns.

Grisaille Tonal painting in shades of one colour, usually grey.

Guilloche A decorative motif consisting of overlapping loops or circles in line.

Hatchment Lozenge-shaped painted heraldic shields of wood or canvas suspended outside houses after a family death, and brought inside a church after the funeral.

Head-stop The termination of an arch carved with a head.

Holy Communion The Protestant equivalent of the Roman Catholic Mass, commemorating the death and sacrifice of Christ for the redemption of humanity.

Inpost A wall bracket supporting one end of an arch.

Kingpost A central vertical column rising from a horizontal rafter to the apex of a timber roof.

Lady Chapel A chapel dedicated to the Virgin Mary.

Lancet A narrow pointed window.

Ledger-stone An incised commemorative floor-stone, often marking the site of a grave or vault underneath.

Lych-gate An arched wooden gateway into a churchyard, originally used to shelter a coffin before a funeral.

Mandorla An upright oval shape housing a holy image.

Mannerism The leading decorative style of 16th-century Italian art.

Mass The central ritual ceremony at the heart of Roman Catholic worship instituted by Christ at the Last Supper and involving the ingestion of bread and wine.

Misericord A hinged seat with decorative carving on the underside, usually found on choir stalls.

Mouchette A curved dagger shape widely used in the early 14th century, and typical of Decorated architecture and design.

Nail-head A common late Norman and Early English decorative motif consisting of a small raised pyramid, usually found in bands or strips.

Nave The main body of a church at the west end, often flanked by aisles.

Ogee Introduced from Arab sources, a double-curved or S-shaped motif widely used in Decorated architecture and design.

Palladian The style associated with the influential north Italian architect and writer Andrea Palladio (*1508-80*) who based his work on Roman prototypes.

Parclose A carved screen around the sides of a chapel.

Pediment A triangular-shaped gable with straight or curved sides widely used in classical architecture and design.

Perpendicular The dominant decorative style of English 15th- and early 16th-century architecture and design, typically light and ornate.

Pieta The image of the dead Christ on his mother's lap after the Crucifixion.

Piscina A small recess usually on the south side of an altar used to wash mass or communion vessels, usually with a drain to the outside of the church.

Polychrome Coloured, usually painted.

Pulpit A raised feature from which the priest conducts services and delivers sermons.

Pulpitum A substantial screen between the nave and the choir in larger churches.

Putto A wingless cherub.

The Regency Literally the years of the Regency of the future King George IV (*1811-20*) but also more broadly referring to the first three decades of the 19th century.

Reredos A carved or painted screen behind an altar.

Retrochoir The space in larger churches behind the choir and the east end.

Reliquary An object housing the relics of saints.

Rococo The asymmetrical decorative style that was popular in the 18th century.

Romanesque The dominant style of late 11th- and 12th-century architecture and design, with round arches.

Rood screen The screen in most pre-Reformation churches on the west side of the chancel arch, carrying representations of Christ on the cross flanked by St John and the Virgin Mary. They were invariably damaged or destroyed during the Reformation.

Roof-boss A projecting stone at the intersection of the ribs of a roof-vault, often elaborately carved with foliage or figurative scenes.

Rose-window A circular window with tracery radiating from or around the centre.

Royal Arms The heraldic coat of arms of the British monarchy, painted on board or canvas or carved in wood.

Sanctuary The east end of the chancel, housing the altar and often protected by low railings.

Sarcophagus A carved stone tomb-chest.

Sedilia Stone seating for priests, often recessed into the wall, usually found in threes on the south side of the chancel.

Spandrel The space on either side of the top of an arch, or between the top of two arches, often filled with decoration.

Stiff-leaf The main type of carved foliage in Early English architecture, with elaborately curved stems and stylised leaves.

Strapwork The main decorative style of 16th- and early 17th-century English decorative art, often with raised strips and richly curved forms.

Tablet A monument suspended on a wall.

Tau-cross A T-shaped cross.

Tracery The ribs inside a screen or window or roof-vault or elsewhere, often used for decorative effect.

Transept The side-extensions of a cruciform church, often flanking a central tower.

Tympanum The space between the horizontal lintel of a doorway or other opening, and the arch above it.

Venetian window A three-light window with a central arched light flanked by two shorter rectangular lights.

The Visitation The meeting between the Virgin Mary and her mother St Ann, after the Annunciation.

Waterleaf A motif widely used in late 12th-century carving, with broad, flat, elegantly simplified decorative leaves.

BIBLIOGRAPHY & REFERENCES

Jonathan Alexander & Paul Binski (eds.), *Age of Chivalry: Art in Plantagenet England 1200-1400*, Weidenfeld & Nicolson/Royal Academy, London, 1987.

J.R. Armstrong, *A History of Sussex*, Phillimore & Co., Chichester, 1974.

H. Belloc, 'The Idea of A Pilgrimage', *Hills and The Sea*, Methuen, London, 1906.

Alan Billings, *Secular Lives, Sacred Hearts: The role of the church in a time of no religion*, SPCK, London, 2004.

Claude Blair, John A. Goodall & Philip Lankester, 'The Winchelsea Tombs Reconsidered', *Church Monuments*, Vol. XV, 2000, pp. 5-31.

Francis Bond, *Fonts and Font Covers* (1908), Waterstone, London, 1985.

Francis Bond, *Screens and Galleries in English Churches*, Oxford University Press, London, 1908.

Francis Bond, *The Chancel of English Churches*, Oxford University Press, London, 1916.

John Bruce, *The History of Brighton with the Latest Improvements, To 1835*, Brighton, 1835.

Frederick Burgess, *English Churchyard Memorials*, Lutterworth Press, London, 1963.

The Revd G.A. Clarkson, 'Notes on Amberley, its Castle, Church etc' *Sussex Archaeological Collections 17*, 1865, pp. 185-239.

William Cobbett, *Rural Rides in Surrey, Kent, and Other Counties* (1853), Penguin Classics, London, 2001.

Nicola Coldstream, *Mason & Sculptors: Medieval Craftsmen*, British Museum Press, London, 1992.

J. Charles Cox, *Pulpits, Lecterns, & Organs in English Churches*, Humphrey Milford/OUP, London, 1915.

J. Charles Cox, *English Church Fittings, Furniture & Accessories*, Batsford, London, 1923.

J. Charles Cox and C.B. Ford, *The Parish Churches of England*, Batsford, London, 1935.

Fred H. Crossley & Frank E. Howard, *English Church Woodwork: a study of craftsmanship during the medieval period A.D. 1250-1550*, Batsford, London, 1917.

Fred H. Crossley, *English Church Monuments A.D. 1150-1550: An Introduction to the Study of Tombs & Effigies of the Medieval Period* (1921), Batsford, London, 1933.

Fred H. Crossley, *English Church Craftsmanship: An Introduction to the Work of the Medieval Period and Some Accounts of Later Developments*, Batsford, London, 1947.

Daniel Defoe, *A Tour Through England and Wales* (1727), J. M. Dent, London, 1929.

Maud F. Drummond-Roberts, *Some Sussex Fonts Photographed and*

Described, Southern Publishers, Brighton, 1935.

Eamon Duffy, *The Stripping of the Altars: Traditional Religion in England 1400-1580*, Yale University Press, New Haven & London, 1992.

George P. Elphick, *Sussex Bells and Belfries*, Phillimore & Co., Chichester, 1970.

Stanley P. Excell, *Sompting Parish Church: A Brief Guide*, Friends of Sompting Church, 1979.

J.C. Fox & C.B. Ford, *The Parish Churches of England* (1935), Batsford, London, 1954.

Nigel Foxell, *Amberley Church – A Critical Appreciation*, Menard Press, London, 2006.

Arthur Gardner, *A Handbook of English Medieval Sculpture*, Cambridge University Press, Cambridge, 1935.

Samuel Gardner, *English Gothic Foliage Sculpture*, Cambridge University Press, Cambridge, 1927.

Edmund W. Gilbert, *Brighton: Old Ocean's Bauble*, Methuen, London, 1954.

Rupert Gunnis, *Dictionary of British Sculptors 1660-1851*, London, 1951.

Rupert Gunnis, *Withyham Parish Church and The Family of Sackville*, Tunbridge Wells, n.d.

R.J.C. Holmes, *Saint Bartholomew's, Brighton: A Description And Guide*, Brighton, 1975.

Peter Howell & Ian Sutton (eds.), *The Faber Guide to Victorian Churches*, Faber and Faber, London, 1989.

W.H. Hudson, *Nature in Downland* (1900), J. M. Dent, London, 1935.

Annabelle Hughes, *A History of North Horsham*, Horsham Parish Council, Horsham, 2000.

Richard Jefferies, *Wild Life in a Southern County* (1879), Thomas Nelson, London, n.d.

Sheila Kaye-Smith, *Weald of Kent and Sussex*, Robert Hale Ltd., London, 1953.

E.V. Lucas, *Highways & Byways in Sussex*, Macmillan & Co., London, 1921.

Richard Marks and Paul Williamson (eds.) *Gothic Art for England 1400-1547*, V&A Publications, London, 2003.

Richard Morris, *Churches in the Landscape*, J. M. Dent, London, 1989.

H.R. Mosse, *The Monumental Effigies of Sussex 1250-1650*, Combridges, Hove, 1933.

I. Nairn & N. Pevsner, *The Buildings of England: Sussex*. Penguin, Harmondsworth 1965.

John Nankivell, *Saint Wilfrid*, SPCK, London, 2002.

Richard Ollard, *The Escape of Charles II after the Battle of Worcester* (1966), Constable, London, 1986.

A.H. Peat & L.C. Halsted, *Churches and Other Antiquities of West Sussex*, Chichester, 1912.

W.D. Peckham, *A Short History of St Peter and St Paul, West Wittering*, West Wittering, 1954.

Richard Ratcliff, *The Story of Boxgrove Priory*, Chichester, 1972.

Eileen Roberts, 'Christopher Webb and the Orchard House Studio', *The Journal of Stained Glass*, Vol.XXV, 2001, pp.79-96.

Malcolm Saville, *The Story of Winchelsea Church*, 22nd edition, Booker & How, Hastings, 2004.

Julie Spraggon, *Puritan Iconoclasm during the English Civil War*, Boydell Press, Woodbridge, 2003.

Anne & John Stamper, *A Short Guide to the Church of St Mary the Virgin, Ringmer E. Sussex*, Ringmer, 1996.

The Revd. Martin Sheppard, *A Short Guide to the Churches of St Mary de Haura, New Shoreham & St Nicholas, Old Shoreham, West Sussex*, New Shoreham, 1980.

The Revd. F. Simpson, *The Churches of Shoreham, Sussex* (1946), The British Publishing Co., Gloucester, 1950.

The Revd. E.N. Staines, *Dear Amberley: A Guide to Amberley and History of the Parish* (1968), St Richard's Press, Chichester, 1998.

Francis W. Steer, *Guide To The Church of Coombes* (1956), The Sussex Historic Churches Trust, Chichester, 1966.

Roy Tricker, *North Stoke Church*, The Churches Conservation Trust, London, 1998.

Victoria County History: Sussex, Vols. 1-9, 1906-87.

John Vigar, *Exploring Sussex Churches*, Meresborough Press, Rainham, 1986.

John Vigar & Mike Robins, *St Andrew's Church, Waterloo Street, Hove*, The Churches Conservation Trust, London, 2005.

A. Katharine Walker, *An Introduction To the Study Of English Fonts: with details of those in Sussex*, Woodward Fawcett & Co., London, 1908.

Simon Watney, 'The lily-crucifixion in late medieval English art', in *Pagans and Christians — Antiquity to the Middle Ages*, Archaeopress, Oxford, Lauren Gilmour (ed.), 2007.

Marcus Whiffen, *Stuart and Georgian Churches Outside London 1603-1837*, Batsford, London, 1948.

Adam White, 'A Biographical Dictionary of London Tomb Sculptors c.1560-1660', *The Walpole Society*, Volume 61, London, 1999.

Erik Woodard, *A Guide to the Parish Church of St Mary the Virgin, Willingdon, in the County of Sussex*, Willingdon, n.d.

Fr. Oliver Woodman, *The Parish Church Of Saint Saviour & Saint Peter, South Street, Eastbourne*, Eastbourne, 2000.

George Zarnecki, Janet Holt & Tristram Holland (eds.) *English Romanesque Art 1066-1200*, Arts Council of Great Britain and Weidenfeld and Nicolson, London, 1984.